The Kinderhook Creature and Beyond:

A Personal Reminiscence

Bruce G. Hallenbeck

This edition published by Small Town Monsters Publishing, LLC in 2022

Copyright © 2022 by Small Town Monsters Publishing, LLC

Author: Bruce G. Hallenbeck

Cover Art: Easton Hawk

Acknowledgments

This book could not have been written without the help of the following individuals: My fellow author and researcher Paul Bartholomew, for his impeccable cryptozoological files and for supplying photographs, newspaper clippings and his wonderful foreword; Paul's brother Robert, whose professional credentials are equally impressive; author Lisa LaMonica, who is an invaluable Hudson Valley researcher in her own right and who helped me with research regarding local ghost stories and supplied me with photographs; William Brann; my mother and father; my sister Susan; my cousin Barry Knights; my cousin Russell Zbierski; *PM Magazine;* Eric Mintel; my friend Susan L; my boyhood chum Jerome Miller; and anyone else who may have slipped through the cracks. With very special thanks to Seth Breedlove, founder of Small Town Monsters; and Heather Moser, my erudite editor.

This book is dedicated with love and respect to my paternal grandmother, Martha May Robertson Hallenbeck, who not only nurtured my creative ambitions but was also a witness to many of the incidents described in this book. Here's to you, Gram, the last of the angels.

Table of Contents

Foreword

Few things are as compelling as a small town and their mysterious secrets. Occult knowledge, fascinating stories, hidden dramas and scary tales.

While often excluded from traditional histories, they form an alternate reality that is only whispered about, many times with a wink and a nudge.

The late legendary Fortean writer John A. Keel referred to these regions as "windows." They are places where the past is thick and seeping with intrigue. The paranormal there becomes normal.

One such location is the tiny town of Kinderhook, New York, located just south of the state Capitol of Albany. Nestled in Northern Columbia County, it is the birthplace of Martin Van Buren, the eighth President of the United States. It is also where Washington Irving penned his classic tale *The Legend of Sleepy Hollow.*

A prominent resident of Kinderhook is Bruce Hallenbeck. For over four decades I have been blessed to call Bruce a friend and colleague. Smart, witty and talented, he is an award- winning author with scores of writing credits. A virtual renaissance man, Bruce has mastered all forms of media from television and radio to newspapers and filmmaking. He is also a joy to be around and to work with.

In the late 1970's, Bruce's grandmother Martha witnessed a hairy creature curled up in the fetal position on her front lawn. As she turned away from her kitchen window, the large creature apparently stood up and walked away, disappearing into the surrounding woods. The incident left Martha stunned and sparked Bruce's investigation into a critter dubbed by newspaper columnist Barney Fowler and the syndicated television program *PM Magazine* as "The Kinderhook Creature."

Research shows that such tales of large hairy bipedal creatures in this area are somewhat common. Native American accounts of the "Wendigo" or of "Stone Giants" are well documented. In fact, explorer Samuel de Champlain wrote about a creature the natives called the "Gougou."

As one delves into these reports, they are exposed to a smorgasbord of unexplained phenomena. A broader picture emerges as seemingly supernatural outbreaks become commonplace.

Strange lights dancing in the sky, parapsychological entities easily passing through physical barriers, haunting eerie screams echoing in the night, strange creatures— large and small— inhabiting our forests.

In recent years the entire landscape of the paranormal has seemingly shifted. Discussions of dark matter, quantum physics and other dimensions that were once ignored or ridiculed have gained scientific credibility.

Bruce Hallenbeck offers the reader a riveting rare personal glimpse into these secret histories and alternate realms which the late astronomer Dr. J. Allen Hynek once referred to as a "parallel reality."

–Paul Bartholomew, August 29th, 2022, author of *Bigfoot Encounters in New York and New England.*

Introduction

I was a monster kid. I grew up in the 1960s, when the "monster" craze was at its zenith. There were magazines like *Famous Monsters of Filmland,* there were monster comic books like *Creepy* and there were those classic Aurora monster models of Dracula, the Wolfman and Frankenstein's monster, among many others. It was a great time to be a young boy with an interest in monsters. When I grew up, I became the author of many books about horror, science fiction and monster movies, such as *The Hammer Vampire, Rock'N'Roll Monsters, Poe Pictures* and so forth, to keep the monster kid tradition alive.

During the process of maturing, however, I also became very interested in "true life" monsters, thanks initially to a book I read in sixth grade called *The Maybe Monsters* by Gardner Soule, a book for young readers that told tantalizing tales of such legendary creatures as Nessie, the Abominable Snowman and Sasquatch. Mind you, I had experienced so-called "real" monsters before that, creatures that couldn't be explained by science, but this book made me realize that I was not the only one seeing them, nor was I imagining them. There were thousands, if not millions of other people who saw them too.

All of this interest was further piqued by the fact that I lived in one of the most haunted places in New York State's Hudson Valley, a little town called Kinderhook, located in northern Columbia County. The name means "Children's Corner" in Dutch, the moniker coined by Hendrick Hudson himself when he sailed up the river on his Dutch ship the Half Moon and was greeted on the shore by a group of Native American children.

It was also in Kinderhook that famed early American author Washington Irving gathered the materials to write *The Sketch Book of Geoffrey Crayon, Gent.,* which contained two iconic stories, *Rip Van*

Winkle and *The Legend of Sleepy Hollow.* Irving stayed in Kinderhook for a time in the early 19ᵗʰ Century, having befriended Martin Van Buren, the eighth President of the United States, who lived in Kinderhook on an estate called Lindenwald. Irving actually wrote the book while he was on a tour of Europe, but the characters were taken from some of his early American acquaintances. Although Kinderhook and Tarrytown, NY, have both claimed the rights to the Sleepy Hollow story, the fact is that Irving based his characters on real Kinderhook residents and placed them in the Tarrytown setting, where he lived, thereby creating something of a friendly feud between the two towns over the years. Turns out both places can claim the story, as Ichabod Crane was based on a real schoolteacher in Kinderhook named Jesse Merwin (who is buried there), Katrina Van Tassell was a Kinderhook gal named Katrina Van Alen, and the legendary Brom Bones was actually Abraham Van Alstyne.

Kinderhook is awash with folklore and history of this kind. The two often intermingle to the point whereby they become virtually indistinguishable from one another. The Headless Horseman. The ghost of Jesse Merwin. The specter of Martin Van Buren. Omens of doom. Relics of death. Kinderhook and nearby environs abound in hauntings and mysteries of all kinds. In fact, new and compelling stories are being added all the time.

Despite growing up in this magical environment – and despite my open-minded attitude towards cryptids in general – I was at first skeptical of such things haunting, quite literally, my own back yard. But then I saw the Kinderhook Blob; I saw the strange man in green; I saw UFOs through our dining room window; and my entire family encountered the infamous "Kinderhook Creature." Could these things have all been part of my writer's imagination?

If I had been the sole witness to all these apparitions and events, I would perhaps think they were all in my mind. In fact, however, that was not the case. Cousins, parents, aunts and uncles and other citizens of the area saw some of them too, or experienced unexplained vocalizations or some sort of paranormal activity.

This book is, in a very real sense, about my beloved paternal grandmother, Martha Robertson Hallenbeck. She and I encountered many of these episodes of what is called "high strangeness" both together and separately. This book is dedicated with the greatest love and respect to her memory. She was one of the wisest, sweetest and kindest people I have ever known. And she was not one to make up stories. If she told you something, you knew it was the truth.

The same goes for this book. You can make of the events contained herein what you will. All I can say is, they're all documented, and, to the best of my knowledge, every word is true.

– 31 August 2022

Chapter One

The Headless Horseman and Washington Irving

A drowsy, dreamy influence seems to hang over the land, and to pervade the very atmosphere. – The Legend of Sleepy Hollow by Washington Irving

When I was a child, I never had to go to grandma's house for Christmas or Thanksgiving, because I lived there. Until I was five years old, my parents lived there too, but they moved down the road when they purchased some land from my mother's mother, who I never knew very well. This was not the case with my father's mother, Martha, who had been taking care of me while my father worked nights and my mother worked days. My grandfather, George Watson Hallenbeck, was still very much alive, but he was working full time and didn't pay a lot of attention to me. As a result, I became closer to my grandmother than to my parents, and when they moved, they asked me if I wanted to go with them or stay with "Gram," as I called her. I opted to stay, and they understood my affection for Gram, for which I will always be eternally grateful. They moved down the road – we still got together all the time, as they were my parents, after all, and there were no hard feelings - and I stayed in the wonderland of the house on McCagg Road, just outside of the village of Kinderhook, with its seven acres of land, mostly woods and fields.

In 1942, my grandparents and their children – my Aunts Shirley and Barbara, my Uncle George and my father – had moved from their home in the little hamlet of West Ghent to a property my grandfather had bought in Kinderhook. For $600 (!) he had purchased 7.2 acres of land on which stood a barn. The house that had previously been there was owned by a family named Anderson, but the house had burned down many years before. I've never been able to find any real details about the Anderson family, but the story I've heard over the years implied that Mr. Anderson himself had intentionally burned down the house, presumably to collect the insurance money. I've never been able to discover whether anyone was injured or killed in that fire, but it's an interesting sidenote to the history of the place where I grew up.

Regardless, the Anderson's barn was converted into a house, and a warmer, cozier home could not be imagined. Most of that warmth was due to my grandmother, a kindly soul who always put her children and grandchildren first. Amazingly, indoor plumbing was never installed until the 1980s, as my grandfather always said that they would have had to blast, as the house was built on shale rock. As it turned out, there was no blasting required when the plumbing was finally installed in 1987. In any case, my grandfather believed in living the simple life, and the fewer the modern conveniences, the better, as far as he was concerned. As for my grandmother and me, well, we didn't necessarily agree, which was why we had the plumbing put in years later. My grandfather was a bit of an eccentric, as I will explain in future chapters.

One of my earliest recollections was watching the Walt Disney version of *The Legend of Sleepy Hollow* on television when I was around three years old. The story enchanted me, and even more so when Gram told me that there was a lot of evidence supporting the idea that Ichabod Crane – and the Headless Horseman – hailed from these parts.

On the way into the village, there is a bridge that spans the Kinderhook Creek. My childhood imagination dictated that it must have been the very bridge upon which Ichabod Crane nearly lost his head in his attempt to escape the Headless Horseman, who was in hot pursuit. Kinderhook lent itself to such fancies, especially in the magical month of October, when Halloween beckoned and leaves crunched underfoot. It was at Halloween, of course, that I imagined the Headless Horseman was near, carrying his Jack-O-Lantern head and ready to decapitate anyone who crossed his path.

Washington Irving, author of "The Legend of Sleepy Hollow"

As it turns out, the Horseman himself was based on some very old legends. For example, Irish folktales tell of the *dullahan,* a type of Irish fairy usually depicted as riding a horse and carrying his head under his arm. The Green Knight in the Arthurian story *Sir Gawain and the Green Knight* was also a headless rider, as was the Scottish horseman called Ewen, who lost his head in a clan battle.

Irving's 1820 story undoubtedly was derived from these sources, but also from Sleepy Hollow itself, a village just outside of Tarrytown in Westchester County, New York. The Headless Horseman or "Headless Hessian," was a part of that area's folklore, involving an unnamed Hessian trooper who was killed in the Battle of White Plains in 1776, decapitated by an American cannonball. The Hessians (German soldiers) fought with the British during that conflict, and the shattered remnants of the head of the unnamed Hessian soldier were left on the battlefield while his fellows carried away his body. He was eventually buried - *sans* head, so the story goes - in the graveyard of the Old Dutch Church of Sleepy Hollow. It is from this resting place that the horseman rides in search of his head – or anyone's – carrying a Jack O'Lantern as both a surrogate head and

Jesse Merwin, the "pattern" for Ichabod Crane

a weapon. The battle of White Plains had taken place on October 28th, so most versions of the story have the horseman riding through the countryside at around Halloween, a most appropriate time.

It is generally accepted that Irving took the characters of his story from actual persons living in Kinderhook and transplanted them to the Tarrytown setting. Rural schoolmaster Jesse Merwin was a friend of both Irving and Martin Van Buren (the eighth President of the United States and a Kinderhook resident), and he taught at a one-room schoolhouse in Kinderhook. That schoolhouse, now called the Ichabod Crane Schoolhouse, is an historic building on Route 9H just south of town, about two miles from where I grew up.

According to a notation by Irving and a certification written in longhand by Van Buren, Merwin was the "pattern" for Ichabod Crane. The certification displayed in the Ichabod Crane Schoolhouse reads in part, "I have known J. Merwin, Esq… for about a third of a century and believe him to be a man of honor and integrity and that he is the same person celebrated in the writings of the Hon. Washington Irving under the character of Ichabod Crane…" – Martin Van Buren, 1846.

As local author/artist Lisa LaMonica – who wrote the books *Haunted Catskills* and *Witches and Warlocks of New York* - puts it, "That letter from Van Buren confirms it. Before Irving even moved down to Tarrytown, the people here in Kinderhook recognized the fact that *The Legend of Sleepy Hollow* was about their neighbors. Ichabod was definitely Jesse Merwin, no two ways about it. You know, I would like to see Kinderhook do more with its literary history. I'd like to see them embrace it more. The *Times Union* did a story last year; they had a woman write about Kinderhook that kind of touched on it a little bit but not enough; such as how Irving was the first American writer to make a living at his craft, that *The Legend of Sleepy Hollow* was the first published American ghost story and that his characters have never faded. That's what's impressive about his story. It continued to be featured in marketing and advertising the world over. It deserves to be celebrated. I think Kinderhook should do more for Halloween. They don't do enough on the actual holiday; they don't do a parade. Hudson (a nearby city) does a big Halloween parade, and there are so many things you could do to increase tourism."

Indeed, the names of Washington Irving's characters and locations permeate Kinderhook and environs. I went to Ichabod Crane High School (of course!), whose basketball team is called "The Riders" after the Headless Horseman; just around the corner from the house where I grew up is the Sleepy Hollow Motel; and so on.

Tarrytown goes all-out for Halloween with town-wide celebrations at Sunnyside (Irving's home), the Sleepy Hollow Cemetery, etc. Kinderhook, while steeped in its old Dutch history, is much more-low key about its Kinderhook/Irving connection. This was not always the case. There was, for example, a Halloween news story covered by our local CBS-TV affiliate for which our high school principal, wearing a costume from the period, played Ichabod Crane in some footage in which he rode a horse by the old Van Alen house. A few years ago on Halloween, I was honored to be asked by the local historical society to read a children's version of *The Legend of Sleepy Hollow* to a group of grade school students in front of the James Vanderpoel House, otherwise known as "The House of History." The conclusion of the story coincided with the arrival of the "real" Headless Horseman (played by a woman), who rode through the fields behind the house and ended up right in front of us. None of the kids were really frightened, although the horse and rider were very impressive - and how she saw where she was going is beyond me, with her head concealed the way it was. Hey, those were Kinderhook kids, and they would have been very disappointed had the Horseman (or woman) not shown up!

Just why the Columbia County Historical Society is generally so reluctant these days to celebrate its connection with the classic story is something I've never understood. If I were the head of that organization, I'd do all I could to promote Ichabod Crane, Katrina Van Tassel, Brom Bones and of course the Headless Horseman. It would work wonders for tourism, especially around Halloween.

I don't think it's a coincidence that I became interested in "monsters," both fictional and (allegedly) real. When someone asks me why I write the types of books I write, I give them Stephen King's stock answer: *What makes you think I have any choice?* Growing up in this wonderfully mysterious atmosphere was perfect for a sensitive, imaginative child like me – which is not to say that I imagined the strange things that have happened to me over the years. Other people can vouch for the veracity of these odd occurrences, although some have passed on since. Yet there are still unusual things happening in this haunted valley and there are always new witnesses.

At any rate, Tarrytown and Kinderhook may continue their "feud" forever, but the fact remains: both places can claim Ichabod Crane and the story of the Headless Horseman. Irving is buried in Sleepy Hollow Cemetery outside Tarrytown, but Merwin is buried in Kinderhook. And some say that he still haunts the place. Ah, but that is a story for our next chapter…

Chapter Two

The Ghosts of Lindenwald and Other Phantoms

Vote for OK – Martin Van Buren's 1840 presidential campaign

Kinderhook, New York, located in the northern part of Columbia County, is the picture-perfect definition of the word "quaint." As of the 2020 census, the population was 8,330. The town of Kinderhook is comprised of two villages, Kinderhook and Valatie. The town also contains the hamlet of Niverville, which is situated next to Kinderhook Lake.

In the year 1609, Hendrick Hudson sailed as far north as what is now Kinderhook on his ship the Half Moon. In Dutch, Kinderhook means "Children's Corner," supposedly because of the Native American children who stood on the bluffs over the Hudson River to watch the Half Moon sailing upstream. The local natives were Mohican, and the early Dutch settlers who arrived in the wake of the Half Moon dealt with them peacefully, for the most part, although there were a few minor skirmishes along the way. Kinderhook was settled by 1651 and established as a town in 1788. It's one of the oldest towns in upstate New York.

The Columbia County Historical Society, which owns several historic buildings as well as a permanent collection of genealogical material, paintings, furniture and textiles, is in the village of Kinderhook. The James Vanderpoel House, also known as The House of History, is located on Broad Street in the village and is a grand old example of Federal architecture that was built in or around 1819. It's currently maintained by the Columbia County Historical Society.

Kinderhook embraces its history in a way that many old towns do not. The Old Columbia Academy, for example, was an early Dutch school established in 1787 that was renamed the Kinderhook Academy in 1834. The former Martin Van Buren Elementary School – where I attended kindergarten through fourth grade – is now an international art gallery called The School, which is a branch of the Jack Shainman Gallery in New York.

Every weekend, Kinderhook has a farmers' market, and people come from miles away to buy Kinderhook apples, which are noted for their sweet taste. The Olde Kinderhook Fair, also known as the Kindercrafters Fair, is an annual arts and crafts fair that takes place every summer in conjunction with the Kinderhook Memorial Library book sale, free tours of the House of History, and live music.

Martin Van Buren, the eighth president of the United States, was born and is buried in Kinderhook. Legend has it that Van Buren popularized the expression "OK," which in his 1840 re-election campaign referred to "Old Kinderhook," his nickname. Whether the story is true or not is a subject that is still debated in academic circles, but what cannot be debated is that his re-election campaign failed, which was certainly not "OK" for him.

Martin Van Buren, eighth President of the United States, who was born in and buried in Kinderhook. Some say he still haunts his old home.

Van Buren's Kinderhook home was called Lindenwald, and it's now a unit of the National Park Service, having been fully restored to its former glory. Van Buren purchased the 36-room mansion during his presidency in 1839, and he returned to it after losing his re-election bid to William Henry Harrison, turning the 125-acre estate into his home and farm from 1841 to his death in 1862 at the age of 79. Designated as a national historic site in 1961, Lindenwald - now officially known as the Martin Van Buren National Historic Site – was also where

Washington Irving wrote portions of *The Sketch Book.* It should come as no surprise, then, that Van Buren's ghost allegedly haunts the estate, which is located on Route 9H one mile south of the village of Kinderhook.

Van Buren named the estate Lindenwald, meaning "linden forest" in German, after the American Linden trees – also known as American Basswood – that lined the Old Post Road, a portion of which still exists near the mansion. Van Buren's shade has allegedly been glimpsed here over the years, perhaps tending to his farm.

Mind you, the tour guides at Lindenwald work for the National Park Service, and perhaps because they wear uniforms that make them look like state troopers, they're very hesitant to discuss anything so disreputable as hauntings. When you get them aside, however, they tend to be a bit more honest and forthright about their own experiences there.

I did just that to get a tour guide to talk to me privately once, and he related that sometimes when they open the place in the mornings, they find that some of the curtains have been taken down during the night. At other times, they discover that certain objects of the house have apparently been washed in a bucket full of water that had been left there. There are also certain occasions when the guides can smell bread cooking in the oven – an old Dutch oven which hasn't been used in over a century. The working theory among the guides, so I was told, is that the spirits of Lindenwald are mostly those of the servants or slaves who used to work there.

Lindenwald, the Martin Van Buren National Historic Site, located in Kinderhook and reputedly haunted.

Although I've never spoken to any actual witnesses, legend has it that Van Buren himself and his favorite son, John, have been seen in the dining room of the old mansion. According to tradition, the old president's spirit wanders all over the estate.

There's also a local tale that Van Buren employed a butler who tended to make "liberal use of the liquor cabinet." Sadly, the butler eventually hanged himself, but that didn't prevent his ghost from haunting the place; several witnesses claim to have seen the ghastly image of his hanging form swinging in the breeze.

Other reports indicate that Aaron Burr may have stayed at the house when he fled from New York City. There was allegedly a secret room where Burr might have stayed. Eyewitnesses over the years claim to have seen Burr's specter wearing a maroon-colored coat with lace ruffles that don't move with the breeze.

Just down the road from Lindenwald, also on Route 9H, stands the Luykas Van Alen House, right next to the original Ichabod Crane schoolhouse. This is the same place where, as you may recall, my high school principal dressed up as Ichabod Crane and rode around for the local TV news crew. Through the years, visitors to the house – another designated National Historic Landmark - have reported strange happenings there. Lori Yarotsky, Executive Director of the Columbia County Historical Society, noted in 2021 for the Albany *Times Union* newspaper that "Ghost stories are in the Hudson Valley's DNA. The human history of this region extends back thousands of years, so there has been ample time for spooky stories to work their way down through the generations."

The property that became the Van Alen House was purchased from the Mohicans in the 1730s by Luykas Van Alen, the patriarch of the family, who wasted no time in having the house built. When Irving stayed in Lindenwald, he befriended the family and got to know all of the Van Alens quite well. Is it the ghost of Katrina Van Alen, *nee* Katrina Van Tassel, which haunts the place? No one seems to know for sure, but Yarotsky said that the most definitive example that she had heard of regarding ghostly encounters in the Van Alen House occurred during one of the public tours of the place. The last tour of the day, which took place at dusk, turned out to be quite memorable when "heavy footsteps were heard across the Great Room's ceiling, emanating from the attic." Needless to say, no one was up there. At least no one who anybody could see.

A few years ago, I spoke to one of the Van Alen House tour guides, and she told me she frequently feels a "presence" in the place. She also told me about the time an African American man to whom she was

The Luykas Van Alen House in Kinderhook, NY, home of Katrina Van Alen, known as Katrina Van Tassel in "The Legend of Sleepy Hollow."

giving a tour entered the house and had to leave almost immediately. He explained to her that he had had an impending, claustrophobic feeling of doom, as if he would be "imprisoned" there, harking back to the days of slavery.

There is an ancient Greek revival house in Kinderhook (the village is full of houses from the 19th Century and earlier) in which guests have reported seeing African slaves working the fields outside the house. It's worth pointing out that, just up the road from the house, there's an old slave burial ground. Guests at the house have also reported hearing rapping and knocking sounds on the walls and doors. Perhaps the slaves are trying to get in?

The former home of Jesse Merwin is still standing and allegedly haunted by his ghost. Long ago, his tombstone was placed face down to make the front step to a private residence. Legend has it that if the stone is disturbed, the Headless Horseman will ride again. The woman who lived there a few years back became curious as to whether it was his tombstone and had it flipped over by a handyman with a crowbar. Sure enough, there was the inscription: "Jesse Merwin." That night, no Headless Horseman was seen, but lightning struck the two maple trees in the front yard and electrified the house. No one has messed with the stone since, and this event occurred in the 1960s.

A few of my friends have had their own ghostly experiences. One friend of mine who I shall refer to as "SL" had interesting experiences while she was growing up in a house that some people considered haunted. I interviewed her for this book, and this is the transcript of that interview:

SL: When I was little, my family moved to Niskayuna (about 38 miles from Kinderhook). This was in 1975, and I was a little kid. I was six or seven when we moved in there. We started hearing what sounded like someone coming in through the front door, walking up the stairs and taking a right into the master bedroom. It was just that same pattern, over and over again. I would hear it, my mom would hear it, my brother was little; and it was never frightening, it was just like, "Oh! Somebody came in the door!" We never saw anything, nothing ever really moved around; it was just the same pattern, the same sound and whether you were upstairs or downstairs, it always sounded like that. When I got older, my mom told me that – not the people who lived there just before us, but the people before that – was a family with three or four kids and they were on their way home and the parents got killed in a car accident. The kids had to move in with relatives. I started thinking about it, and thinking, "What if it's the parents who are coming home and looking for the kids?" I started thinking about it that way, and it was almost uncanny that it seemed like there was something there that was parental, not scary, nothing

17

that frightened us. As time went by, as my brother and I got older, it stopped. I kind of forgot about it for a while. We lived in the house for 17 years; I was in college when my mom moved out of that house. The people who moved in were the family who lived two doors down. They loved the neighborhood, but their house was small, and they wanted a bigger house because they had kids. The kids were elementary or junior high age, so they just wanted to move into someplace bigger. I just half-jokingly said something to this woman when I saw her later on, "Do you ever hear anything in the house?" She said, "Hear what?" And I said, "Do you ever hear any strange noises?" And she said, "Yeah, we hear the front door open, and we hear somebody walk up the stairs and take a right and go into the master bedroom." And I thought, "My gosh, there are little kids in the house again!" She said to me, "I thought about that because when I was growing up, my friend lived in this house and her parents died in a car accident." Turns out she was friends with the kids in that family, and I didn't know that. She said, "I always thought it was them coming home." It was just so strange that she and I came to the same conclusion. Even my dad heard it when I was a kid. Nobody was scared; it seemed friendly. There was a constant presence there, probably until I was close to 15 or 16 and my brother would have been 13. So, I don't know, maybe they thought we were grown enough to take care of ourselves… that was comforting. In the house I grew up in, there was one time when I went downstairs in the middle of the night to get cereal and I saw a glowing skeleton, so I ran back upstairs! That was the only time I ever saw anything in that house that freaked the hell out of me.

BGH: Do you think that was your childhood imagination?

SL: Probably. That one I don't have any sense of being real. I was probably 12 or 13. Maybe I watched something scary on TV, and I was suggestible.

The City of Hudson is the county seat of Columbia County. Named after Hendrick Hudson, who sailed up what is now the Hudson River in his ship the Half Moon, the city eventually became a port of call for sailors, as well as prostitutes, so Hudson has a rather checkered past. Also, like its neighbor Kinderhook, which is about twelve miles away, it has its share of hauntings.

These days, Hudson is a respectable and upscale haven for refugees from New York City, but the old haunts are still there. One of the best-known haunted houses in Hudson is located on Warren Street, the city's main drag. A house that was already old when it was purchased by Byron and Mabel Parker in 1904, it was bought by a family named Dietz after Mabel Parker – whose husband predeceased her – passed away after a long illness. When Mr. and Mrs. Jay Dietz moved in, it seemed like a very peaceful place. That was soon to change, however.

The story of the Dietz haunting was featured in a book by the famed paranormal author Hans Holzer in his 1997 book *Ghosts: True Encounters with the World Beyond.* Holzer personally investigated the case and interviewed Mr. and Mrs. Dietz, who related to him that, prior to their living in the house, some tenants would not sleep in one of the upstairs bedrooms, claiming there was something "uncanny" about it. The Dietzes were not interested in such stories, however, and paid no attention to them – until they experienced some events they couldn't explain.

At times, they would hear footsteps trudging up and down the stairs when no one else was there, until the footsteps stopped in the upstairs hallway. They heard these unexplained noises many times, and so did Mrs. Dietz's mother, who resided there with them. One year just before Christmas, Mrs. Dietz was in the hallway "attending to some sewing" while her husband was in the bathroom, when she heard what she thought was her husband walking down the hall. Then she realized that he was still in the bathroom.

A few nights later, Mrs. Dietz felt that there was someone in the bedroom with her – besides her husband, that is. And a few nights after that, she was awakened by someone – or some*thing* – pulling at her blanket from the foot of her bed. When she sat up, it suddenly stopped.

On another occasion, she felt her blanket being pulled off. More than once, after turning out the lights in the bedroom, she felt the presence of someone – again, not her husband – standing next to the bed, looking down at her. Holzer, the author of more than 100 books on the paranormal and a professor of parapsychology at the New York Institute of Technology, was called in and met the Dietz family at their house. Mrs. Dietz and her mother told him that both women – in their respective rooms – were awakened at approximately 5:00 in the morning by the sound of heavy, slow footsteps dragging up the stairs, going down the hallway and suddenly stopping.

Mrs. Dietz pointed out that these particular footsteps sounded different from the others they had heard: "It sounded as if a very sick person was dragging her way up the stairs," she told Holzer, "trying not to fall but determined to get there, nevertheless. It sounded as if someone very tired was coming home."

Perhaps – just perhaps – Mabel Parker, who was known as something of a homebody, was returning from the hospital to sleep in her own bed. Holzer passed away some years ago and was never able to return to the Dietz home, so we'll never know for sure.

Author/artist Lisa LaMonica had similar experiences when she lived at her brother's house in Hudson many years ago. She told me, "It was a house where the upstairs apartment was empty. And you could hear somebody walking around, plain as day, on some nights. My mother was in the den once and I asked her, 'Why are they letting the kids run around at eleven o'clock at night?' And my mother said, 'Holly doesn't live up there anymore.' I heard somebody running around up there two nights in a row. I heard it as plain as day."

LaMonica believes that one of the painters of the Hudson River School – a romantic art movement of the 19th Century – either bought or built the house. "If you were on the main floor," she continued "…the basement area was like a den and where the kitchen was…you'd get up in the morning, and it would sound like someone was making a meal in the kitchen. This went on for a long time."

Sutherland Crypt: The Sutherland family crypt where Caroline Sutherland was interred in a glass coffin.

LaMonica also related a local ghost story that is particularly creepy. It had to do with a family called the Sutherlands, who placed one of their own in a glass coffin when she died. The coffin was on view for many years in a cemetery vault between the villages of Chatham and Chatham Center, roughly six miles from Kinderhook. "On a certain June night," LaMonica told me, "people would see this woman on the anniversary of her wedding. People would see her occasionally at night picking flowers in a field. Apparently, she died in childbirth, and I think the baby died as well. They were both buried in these glass coffins. In the early years of the 20th Century, there was no embalming and yet she was perfectly preserved in that glass coffin, as was the rose she was holding. She was in a crypt, and the door had fallen off, so people started turning up to see the coffin; there was a doctor who lived in Chatham Center who went to look at it, and he said her preservation was an anomaly, there was no explanation for it.

"They ended up moving her coffin to Chatham Center and she's in that cemetery now. But he was a medical doctor who went to see for himself in the late 1950s or early 1960s and he could see her plain as day, with the rose and everything. She was behind that glass pane, and she was perfectly preserved."

LaMonica interviewed a woman named Yolanda (I'm omitting her surname) who claimed to have seen the specter of the Sutherland woman about twenty-five years ago. Yolanda related, "My husband and I were coming back…on Thomas Road. My husband was driving, and I was in the passenger's seat… around midnight, a summer night, and the car lights picked up a woman in the middle of a field to my right, who seemed to be picking flowers. The field was full of wildflowers. It was just a second, she looked up… was young and dressed in bright colors. The car lights quickly passed her, and I could no longer see her nor the field because of the darkness."

LaMonica related to me another story that she had researched, having to do with a house in Ghent, just a few miles from Kinderhook. In 1984, a well-to-do couple from New York City purchased a ten-room 1720 colonial in the hamlet of Ghent. With 350 acres of land, it was perfect for their purposes, a real getaway from the hustle and bustle of the city.

"The Sutherland Ghost"
Caroline Sutherland

Something there was not "quite right," though. Shortly after moving in, the couple heard weird noises (including voices) and furniture being moved. At first, they tried to pooh-pooh the incidents, but a guest from New Jersey who was staying in one of the three bedrooms told them that, when he awoke during the night, he saw a skeletal figure standing near the foot of the bed.

The couple's relatives, visiting from Connecticut and staying in the same bedroom, related that they heard footsteps approaching their door in the middle of the night. They felt very uncomfortable about returning there for another stay.

As nearly anyone from Ghent will tell you, that estate, known as Broadstairs, has a colorful history. In 1791, Sheriff Cornelius Hogeboom was shot dead there. He was the sheriff of the town and was attempting to serve a writ of eviction – just doing his job, as it were – when the current occupant murdered him. Hogeboom, who had served as an army captain during the Revolutionary War, became the first known law enforcement officer to be killed in the line of duty in the United States.

A hundred years after that, a farmer named Schmidt – who was working at Broadstairs – beat his stepson to death with a hammer. He was also accused of murdering another individual, whose body was found buried in the cellar. As LaMonica observed, "Broadstairs may have occupants who never left."

As for Kinderhook, LaMonica – a former resident of the village – thinks it is indeed a haunted place. "I would say there's something mystical and magical and spooky about it," she told me. "There's something in the air, and I think it has to do with the Headless Horseman. The old house on Broad Street is supposedly haunted by an apparition that appears just before a war breaks out. It was allegedly seen there at a dinner party just before Pearl Harbor was attacked. Who it is, no one seems to know, but it's an omen of war and death."

After my father retired from his job as president of a wholesale plumbing company, he became "Mr. Fix-It," traveling around town repairing furnaces, bathrooms and, well, you name it, often for little old ladies who couldn't do it themselves. One such little old lady owned a house on Route 203 between Kinderhook and nearby Chatham. The house was reputedly haunted and one day when my father arrived for work, the little old lady having gone somewhere, he saw that the rocking chair on the porch was rocking all by itself, with no human agency present.

That made him pretty uneasy, but he had to work in the basement, so he took the key left for him, went inside and spent that entire afternoon with the uneasy feeling that someone – or some *thing* – was watching him. My father is not easily frightened, but on that occasion, he fully admitted to breathing a sigh of relief when his work there was done.

Broadstairs, an estate in Ghent, NY, which may have ghostly occupants to this day.

Again, I must relate some personal anecdotes. My grandfather, who slept in a separate bedroom from my grandmother, had a nightmare around the time of his retirement

23

(he had worked in the Ichabod Crane Central School district for many years) that disturbed him so much, he moved out. Let me explain.

He told us that he had dreamed there was a "shadow" that pulled him into the bedroom wall. He was obviously quite bothered by the dream even as he was telling us about it, and he was rarely bothered by that sort of thing. Aside from some interesting and old-fashioned beliefs – more on those later – he was a very pragmatic sort of person. He pretty much ignored me and my interests, leaving it to my grandmother to raise me. And so, he had no interest in the paranormal or in cryptozoology.

Shortly after having the dream, he moved most of his belongings from his bedroom to a tent he erected in the woods on the property. By that time, he had retired from his job and most people assumed he wanted to retire surrounded by the forest, as it were. But my grandmother and I felt that his nightmare had something to do with him pitching his tent in the woods. He lived in that tent until he was 80 years old, at which point he decided to build himself a little cabin near where he had pitched his tent. He never returned to his old bedroom.

My grandfather was quite an eccentric character. In addition to being a consummate woodsman, he was a talented "primitive" artist, working in chalk and pastels, among other media. He would sketch pretty much anything; when my wife, Rosa, first moved into the house, we went up to what we affectionately call "the little house on the prairie," i.e. my grandfather's cabin, and she found dead birds and even one dead bat that he had kept around for sketching.

The thing that always impressed me, though, was that this very skeptical fellow had been so traumatized by a dream that he moved out of his own house.

Back in the 1970s, my grandmother and I were having dinner in her dining room when a dish of corn suddenly decided to move itself along the table. It moved to the very edge of the table and stopped suddenly, just before it would have fallen off onto the floor. She and I looked at each other in wonderment, then started to laugh. It was only one of many strange things that happened to both of us.

One of the most puzzling things that ever occurred in my grandparents' house concerned my grandmother's coleus plant. She loved plants and she had quite a green thumb when it came to growing them. Her coleus plant sat in the dining room in the middle of a depression in a metal table, surrounded by two higher points of the table. My grandmother was sitting in the living room, from which she could see the entire dining room, when I walked past the metal table into the kitchen. As I was in the kitchen, I heard something crash. I hurried back into the dining room to see what had fallen, and I saw the pot in which the coleus plant had been standing straight up on the floor. The thing was that the coleus plant was not in it anymore. It was gone. Nor was there any spilled dirt on the floor.

I asked my grandmother if she had seen what had happened. She said she saw the pot, with the plant still in it, rise from its spot in the center of the table, move to the side and fall to the floor. She said it didn't just fall, it rose first, then fell.

We searched everywhere for the coleus plant. We never found it. It had simply vanished, as though it had been teleported into some other dimension. Nor was there a speck of dirt on the floor. It was one of the most mysterious things that ever happened to me, and my grandmother wondered to her dying day what had happened to it. It was one for Sherlock Holmes.

On another occasion, a friend of mine was visiting me in my room upstairs. We were listening to records and chatting, when we both heard someone clomping up the stairs. We waited for someone to appear in the doorway, which was open. No one did. We looked outside in the hallway for whomever may have walked up the stairs. There was no one there.

Many years later, when my then-girlfriend and I stayed at the house, she insisted on sleeping on the side of the bed nearest the window, as she thought she heard sounds in my grandfather's old room. The fact is, as previously noted, my grandfather had moved out of his room a few years before and had pitched a tent on a wooded spot of the property. Having retired from his job at the Ichabod Crane

Central School, where he had been the building superintendent, he decided to get back to nature. As he and Gram had long been, shall we say, uncommunicative with each other, he decided to spend the rest of his days in his beloved outdoors – mostly – where he took up painting and drawing. He had the best of both worlds, mind you: he would come in for meals, which Gram would dutifully prepare for him.

So, if my girlfriend heard noises in my grandfather's old bedroom, they weren't made by him. She also told me that when she went downstairs at night to go to the bathroom, she could see through the chinks in the stairs that the bathroom light was on. When she reached the bathroom under the stairs, the light was off. Little things like that happened all the time.

I certainly never felt threatened by any of these incidents, but they could be a bit unsettling at times. Gram's reaction was more one of suppressed amusement than fear; her sense of humor was legendary, and she always said she wanted to live in a haunted house. "You do!" I told her, and she found that amusing too.

Gram passed away peacefully in her own home, in her own bed, in 1993 at the age of 87. A few weeks before she died, she told me of a strange dream she'd had, although she wasn't sure it was a dream: she said she thought she woke up in bed, and there was a beam of light flashing down into the bedroom. And then, she said, "the room was full of people." I asked her if they were people she recognized and she said she wasn't sure, as she couldn't see them very clearly. Oddly, my sister Susan, who lives just down the road in view of my grandparents' house, said she saw what looked like 'lightning' over the house at around the same time. She said it was just over that house and nowhere else, as far as she could tell.

Shortly after Gram passed away, my sister told me that she found a message from her on her phone. She played it for me, and it was definitely Gram's voice. The voice said, "I was just wondering if you were okay." My sister thought perhaps it was a leftover message that had only been partly erased. Perhaps.

After Gram left this world, I was very sad indeed. I missed her terribly. This was compounded, perhaps, by the fact that I was still living in her house, taking care of it and paying taxes until the family decided what to do with it. My grandfather had had a heart attack at the end of 1991, and he was living with my parents now at their place. So, I was all alone in Gram's house.

During the next few months, I felt as if I were wandering in Limbo. There were times when, totally out of the blue, tears would start streaming down my face. I could be anywhere when that feeling of emptiness overtook me; at times I would be sitting alone in a restaurant when I would unexpectedly start to become emotional. I tried not to let anyone see the tears that ran down my cheeks.

As the holidays approached that year, my melancholia grew. I kept looking for signs that Gram was still around, somewhere, somehow. Perhaps she whispered in the breeze, perhaps she could be seen if I looked carefully into her room. I couldn't believe she was gone. I thought that, like the mountains and the sea, she would be here forever.

One day, as I sat outside in a lawn chair, I thought I saw her in her bedroom window. That was probably because I desperately wanted to see her. Perhaps it was the reflection of a cloud moving across the window, but I wanted it to be her.

Then, on Thanksgiving Day, something remarkable happened. Months before, while Gram was still with us, a female friend of mine had dinner with us and asked if she could take a couple of flowers from Gram's table and plant them just outside the dining room window. This she did, and then autumn came, and the flowers wilted and died. Apparently.

On Thanksgiving morning that year, it was ten degrees Fahrenheit. All the ground was barren, much of it frozen. Yet outside the dining room window, those flowers that my friend had planted months before suddenly bloomed. I happened to see them when I was eating breakfast. I couldn't believe it. I went outside to make sure I wasn't seeing things. Then, for further proof, I took photos of those flowers, those flowers that were in full bloom on the coldest day of the season so far, and then I took photos of the brown, dead grass that covered the lawn. It was extraordinary. If ever I saw a sign from beyond, that was it.

Things were quiet for some time after that until I met my future wife, Rosa, at the offices of The Rensselaer Beacon newspaper, where I was the editor and she was the art director. We had something of a whirlwind romance, and she ended up moving into the old homestead with me. One day, she noted that, while doing some work upstairs, she had seen an old lady wearing an apron as she walked into my grandmother's old bedroom. She said she had seen her only for an instant, but she described Gram perfectly: white hair, glasses, wearing an apron. She even described one of Gram's favorite aprons that she tended to wear nearly every day. At that point, she hadn't even seen a good photograph of her, so I found her description to be extraordinarily accurate. Rosa wasn't rattled by the incident; in fact, she felt quite comforted by it, as we both knew who it was.

In fact, she pointed out to me from the very beginning that she felt a very warm, welcoming presence in the house. That would be Gram, for sure. She was always warm and welcoming to everyone.

When we were first together, Rosa and I – both of whom had been single for many years – tended to get in each other's way at times, as we both had very specific ways of doing things. This sometimes led to friction, and one evening, we got into a verbal argument in Gram's room – I truly can't remember what it was about now – and Rosa ended up taking off in her car. I was quite upset, and I went outside to sit at the picnic table and think about what had just occurred.

As I sat there in the darkness, I happened to look up at the window of Gram's old room and I noticed something very odd: a red light enveloped the entire bedroom, lighting up everything within it. I could clearly see the bed, some bric-a-brac and pretty much everything else.

After getting over the initial shock – there was no red light in my grandmother's room that could account for this – I tried to think of some rational explanation. I watched when some cars drove by to see if their taillights could possibly be reflecting in the second-story window. That, of course, was ridiculous. Even if they had reflected on the second floor – which they didn't – the lights from the cars would certainly not have lit up the entire room.

What really gave me the creeps, though, was what happened next. As I continued to stare at the window, the red light suddenly flickered and *went out.* It was just as if someone had unscrewed a light bulb and taken it out of its socket. And the room was suddenly plunged into pitch darkness.

The hairs stood up on the back of my neck as I contemplated this. I didn't know what to think. I had witnessed all this very plainly. I was, in fact, in a slightly heightened state of awareness because of the argument Rosa and I had, and I knew I wasn't hallucinating. I decided to go into the house to investigate.

It was with quite a bit of trepidation that I walked inside the house, the downstairs of which was fully lighted. I slowly and rather surreptitiously walked up the stairs to enter Gram's old bedroom. When I entered the room was completely dark. I turned on the one light in the room – a white 60-watt bulb – and didn't see anything out of place. Indeed, the room was full of the bric-a-brac that I had seen from my seat at the picnic table, that I had viewed very clearly under the glow of a red light.

When Rosa came home not long afterwards, we resolved our little disagreement, and I told her about my creepy experience. Despite her own experiences, Rosa tends to be quite skeptical about such things, but she found this account of mine to be quite compelling – and she could see how mystified I was by it. She and I had recently befriended David J Pitkin, author of the book *New England Ghosts,* and we told him about my experience. He explained that, in the world of the paranormal, red was the color of anger: perhaps the red light was an expression of Gram's anger about Rosa and me having an argument in her old room?

Rosa and I got to know Pitkin quite well that year, and he invited us up to an investigation of a haunting at an elementary school in Saratoga Springs, New York, home of the Saratoga Racetrack and a haven of the well-to-do. The school was reputedly haunted by a few different spirits, according to both staff and students. The ghost of a deceased janitor supposedly still occupied the boiler room downstairs; at times people saw only his legs! One recently hired staff member saw a picture of the late janitor for the first time in one of the old school yearbooks and pointed out that she had seen the man himself just a few days previously…

Pitkin guided Rosa and me around the school, and when we got to the auditorium, we noticed that the closer we got to the stage, the colder it got. Pitkin pointed out that the stage had been built over an old colonial cemetery, which gave us an additional chill.

This was also the first time we ever heard of "zips," moving objects seen out of the corner of the eye that seemed to vanish when one tried to look at them directly. While that seemed like a bit of a stretch to me – and neither Rosa nor I saw any – it still made for a very interesting day at the school.

Several years later, I awoke at home in the middle of the night – something I do with great frequency – and saw that two of my VHS tapes were no longer on the bookshelf where they had been, but were now on the floor, standing upright next to each other. I thought this was quite odd, to say the least. Rosa half-heartedly suggested that maybe a mouse had moved them, but we both knew how unlikely that was. And even if a mouse had been able to move the tapes, would it have set them up on end right next to each other? I wish I could recall what tapes they were; perhaps there was some significance regarding the titles, but, alas, my memory of them has been lost to time.

I like to think that Gram is still with us, just not in a way that she can be seen (usually). As of this writing, Rosa and I still live in the old house, and there are times when we can sense that Gram is watching over us, wanting us to succeed in our various endeavors, with her hand on our shoulders, guiding us. My fervent hope is that someday, when it's my turn to see the beam of light shining through the ceiling and my room full of people, that the person standing in front of them will be dear Gram.

Home of the author's paternal grandparents, site of many a strange happening.

Chapter Three

Dig It, Man: Fairies and Other Entities

On nearer approach, he was still more surprised at the singularity of the stranger's appearance. He was a short, square-built old fellow with thick bushy hair and a grizzled beard. His dress was of the antique Dutch fashion... – Rip Van Winkle by Washington Irving

Strange entities have always been said to haunt the mountains, valleys and woodlands of the Hudson Valley. I'm not talking now about spirits of the dead, but rather about spirits of nature. A sprite is a supernatural entity in European folklore, the mythology of which was transported to the New World with the first settlers. Sprites are often said to be elementals, spirits of earth, air, fire and water. They may take many forms, most often as "little people" or fairies, but at other times may be more like the "sylphs" of legend, more or less invisible beings of air or water.

When I was a child, I may have encountered an elemental in the woods behind my grandparents' house. It was during summer vacation, and I was nine or ten years old. My younger cousin Chari (pronounced "Sherry") and I were playing on top of the wooded hill behind the house, as we were wont to do. We were on the outskirts of the property on the highest point on the hill, which adjoined a neighbor's land. That area was covered in pine trees, some of which grew to a great height.

It was late in the day, just before sunset, when we both heard a high-pitched whistling sound. It seemed to be nearby, and I turned quickly in the direction from which I felt the sound had come. Much to my surprise – and shock – I saw a white object seemingly peering at me from behind one of the huge old pine trees. I say it was "peering" at me, but it had no eyes that I could see. I simply *felt* that it saw me. It looked like an amorphous, bluish white "blob," and its head – if that's what it was – was high up against the tree's trunk, meaning that, whatever it was, it was quite sizable. I would say the "head" was about the size of a beach ball. Whatever it was, it scared the bejeepers out of me.

The closest I can get to describing the entity is that it looked something like Casper the Friendly Ghost of animated cartoon fame. Its "head" was bulbous, big and round, with that weird bluish tint to it. My cousin was too afraid to turn and look; I told her we should both get out of the woods *now* and we ran down the hill with great speed – the kind of headlong speed that only kids possess – and we never looked back.

I should point out here that the "blob" – as I later came to call it - appeared near a natural spring in the woods, and that my grandfather was a "water witch," or dowser. Dowsing is an old and distinguished tradition, a type of divination to locate water underneath the ground. It involves using a y-shaped twig or rod, usually called a dowsing rod or a witching rod, and if the rod points down to a specific location with no assistance from the dowser, there is usually ground water there.

My grandfather, was, as I have said, an interesting character. A true man of the woods, he dabbled in art – mostly paintings of natural scenes – and, although he was skeptical of most aspects of the paranormal, his belief in dowsing was absolute. And with good reason: in 1964, during a summer of terrible drought, he found water underneath the woods on the property through dowsing with a clothes hanger that he had altered into a "y" shape.

The spring that we had used for water was nearly dry that year and finding more water underground was a godsend. The water that my grandfather turned up was more than enough; once he dug into the ground there, the water spurted out, and before long, had become a pond that was about six feet wide. It attracted frogs and mayflies by the dozens and quickly became a part of the forest ecosystem.

I point this out because many paranormal events are associated in one way or another with underground springs. Native Americans have long associated water with supernatural power. Paranormal entities such as water sprites are considered in many cultures to be the elemental spirits of water, protecting the life that swarms within it. Some researchers contend that water fuels paranormal activity by supplying entities with the energy they need to manifest themselves physically. While there is of course no proof of this theory, I've always found it interesting that many of the unexplained experiences I've had have been in the vicinity of the underground water in the woods.

It was shortly after my grandfather had dug the pond, on a sunny August afternoon a few days before my twelfth birthday, when my boyhood chum Jerome Miller was down in the woods preparing the latest "monster tour." The monster tour was a tradition that I had started, along with my older cousin Russ and his friend Mike, on my eighth birthday, in which I would guide my family through certain paths in the woods from which my cousins, dressed in monster masks, would jump out and scare them. Everyone enjoyed the first monster tour so much – despite the fact that, at one point, I got lost on one of the trails – that it became a yearly tradition of laughs and "screams."

Jerome was good at building things, so he took the monster tour a step further and put together some cables down in the woods that "creatures" could sail down the hill on if someone – me, of course – stepped on the stick to which the cables were attached. Then a "creature" made of old clothes sewn together with a monster mask for a head would fly at our guests, startling them and making them laugh out loud at, as the carnival barkers used to say, "one and the same time."

Jerome was preparing one of these gags in the woods while I went up to the house to use the facilities, as I recall. When I walked out the back door, Jerome was almost at the doorstep, running up to the house and looking as pale as … well, a ghost.

Upon catching his breath, Jerome told me that he had just seen a "big white blob" gliding down the hill towards him. He noted that it had frightened him so badly he had jumped clear over the six-foot wide pond that was down there near the spring. Then he had made a mad dash for the house.

My first thought was that Jerome was pulling my leg; after all, it was quite a coincidence that he was preparing the monster tour and saw something "monstrous" and real himself. Then it occurred to me that I had never told him about the similar "blob" that I had seen down there a few years before. I suggested that maybe we should go down into the woods and attempt to track down this "blob."

And so, the two of us, pitchforks in hand – and what good they would be against an ephemeral "blob" I have no idea, but we probably got the idea from those outraged villagers in Frankenstein movies – set out for the woods. And guess what? We saw something.

As we were tramping through the fallen leaves and underbrush of the forest floor, Jerome suddenly stopped dead and pointed straight ahead without saying a word. I looked in the direction his finger was pointing, and I saw "it" for the second time in my life. I saw a large white shape that seemed to hover in the trees, in broad daylight on that sunny afternoon.

Our pre-adolescent bravado left us immediately. I shouted, "My gosh, let's get out of here!" and like most eleven or twelve-year-old boys when confronted with the unknown, we dropped our weapons, turned tail and ran.

Jerome and I talked about what we had seen when we got back to the house. We didn't know exactly what it was, but we sure knew it was weird. That's when I told him about what I'd seen a few years before, and how it looked like the same thing. And that's when we christened it "the blob."

That was not the end of the blob's exploits. Sightings of the entity spanned generations, as it turned out. More than 16 years later, two of my younger cousins saw something in the woods, and here the story becomes even stranger. I had never told my cousins Barry (Chari's brother) or Russell about my childhood "blob" sightings, but that didn't prevent them from seeing it some 16 years later.

The two of them had been in a lean-to they had constructed in the woods. They were both teenagers at the time and they spent a lot of time down there at the bottom of the hill, sitting around campfires and talking about the usual teenage boy problems: girls, cars, the latest movies, "important" things like that. Again, it was a fine sunny afternoon when they saw... something.

The lean-to was near the same spot where Jerome and I had seen the blob when we were kids. Barry and Russell later told me they had been startled by a "white, almost bell-shaped kind of thing" that glided down the hill towards the lean-to. Now here's the interesting part: Barry, who is Protestant, saw the amorphous bell-shaped thing that Jerome and I had seen gliding down the hill.

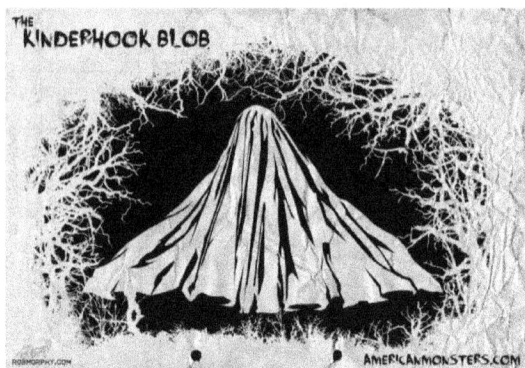

Interpretation of The Kinderhook Blob, courtesy of artist Rob Morphy.

Russell, who is Catholic, saw the Virgin Mary gliding down the hill.

Whatever my cousins saw, they took off much as Jerome and I had done years before. Why did they see two different things? Could what they saw have been colored by their religion? Russell went to Catholic school and was well-versed in sightings of the Virgin Mary, which happen with a fair amount of frequency throughout the Catholic world. Could those sightings be the result of cultural expectations? In other words, could the blob have an objective reality the appearance of which was influenced by one's religious beliefs?

36

Russell agreed with Barry that the object was white. And he agreed that it glided down the hill. But, to him, the shape the entity took was that of the Virgin Mary. I found this to be fascinating, and still do, to this day.

Yet even that was not the end of the story. Another decade and a half or so later, my father was out on his tractor doing some work on his property, just down the road from my grandparents' house, when he said he saw something "big and white" flying over his head against the clear blue sky. He saw it only for a second before it vanished into the woods, but he described it as looking like a "shmoo," a cartoon character created by Al Capp in the classic comic strip *L'il Abner*. A shmoo was supposedly a white, amorphous entity – a "blob," in fact – that dwelled in the forest. My father had used his own frame of reference to describe what was essentially the same thing that had been seen by my friend Jerome, my cousins and myself.

In recent years, what has come to be called the Kinderhook Blob has taken on a life of its own. There are several websites devoted to it and there's even a drawing of it one can purchase on e-bay for 20 cents! I must say, it warms the cockles of my heart to know that something I saw when I was a young lad has influenced generations of cryptid hunters. The online illustrations run from the sublime (a bell-shaped thing) to the ridiculous (a cartoon ghost). Apparently, the information on these "blob blogs" (one of which is called "The Kinderhook Blob") was taken from a couple of previous publications in which I mentioned my family's sightings. Some of the details they report are incorrect, but the general gist is there.

And, according to a couple of these sites, the blob has been seen as recently as 2017, when "two men (town locals Owen Farley and Anthony Malanowski) were on a late-night walk through the woods. The pair claimed that the temperature around them dropped sharply right before the Blob came shooting out between the trees. This sighting cited the height of the creature as upwards of seven feet tall, and again said it was making a screeching or whistling sound," according to themorbidlibrary.com. Supposedly, it floated towards them at high speed, causing them to run away in fear. Sound familiar?

As if that weren't enough to keep the dear old Kinderhook Blob in the public consciousness, a fellow who calls himself (or his company) Ed Metazoo offers his own visualization of the blob on his 2022 "caster's cup" – also a hologram! - which sells for $95 on e-bay. Just for the record, Metazoo also makes the same sort of item based on the "Ohio Grassman," a kind of sasquatch from that state, in his series of collector's items. Who knew?

Now back to dear old Washington Irving--where would we be without him? Everybody knows his story *Rip Van Winkle,* in which an early American colonist is challenged to play a game of nine-pins by the diminutive "spirits" of Hendrick Hudson and his crew of the ship The Half Moon. Rip accepts some of their liquor, drinks it and falls asleep, not awakening for twenty years, by which time the thirteen colonies have separated from Great Britain to form the United States of America. Irving's whimsical fantasy was inspired by ancient tales of "fairy abductions" in which the Little People abduct human beings into the Land of Fairie, where time has no meaning.

More specifically, Irving may have based his story on a folktale from the Orkney Islands of Scotland, where there is a burial mound adjacent to an ancient Neolithic stone circle called the Ring of Brodgar. In that tale, a drunken fiddler on his way home hears otherworldly music issuing from beneath the mound. Attracted by the sound, the man finds his way into the mound and discovers trolls and elves having a wild gathering – as trolls and elves are given to do. The man is forced to stay there and play his fiddle for them to dance for what seems to be two hours, then makes his way home. When he arrives there, he discovers that 50 years have passed. It's something of a horror story when you think about it. Irving's father came from the Orkneys, and Irving may well have heard the story when he was a child.

Native Americans had their own legends of "little people" that were amazingly like those of Celtic lands and other European regions.

This makes one wonder if there is more to these stories than meets the eye. The Cree, for example, believed in a dwarf-sized race of tricksters they called the Mannegishi – small humanoids with slim arms, lanky legs and oversized, noseless heads. The Mannegishi were said to have lived between rocks in the rapids of rivers, where they were thought to have delighted in crawling out of the rocks to capsize canoes, dragging the boaters to their watery deaths.

Algonquin tribes told of the Memegwesi, dwarfs with hairy faces who dwelled on riverbanks. The Memegwesi often traveled in groups (gangs?) and supposedly appeared only to those of "pure mind," which generally indicated they appeared mainly to children. The similarities to the Celtic legends of fairies are quite striking. From where could such stories arise?

The Algonquin, Abenaki, Mohican, Ojibwe and Wampanoag tribes also spoke of the pukwudgie, small, enchanted people of the forest who were, again, remarkably similar to European tales of fairies, gnomes and leprechauns. Tales of the pukwudgies were told throughout the northeastern United States as well as throughout Canada and the Great Lakes region. Pukwudgies could be evil and dangerous, but only to those who had no respect for them – just as the fairies in Celtic countries insisted on being referred to by ordinary mortals as "The Good People" or they would play mischievous tricks on them. Like the fairies, the pukwudgies were capricious creatures who generally played harmless pranks, but at a whim might kidnap children – shades of the "changeling" legends in British and Celtic folklore – or play downright evil tricks on humans. Usually described as being roughly knee-high to ordinary folks, or even smaller, the name pukwudgie literally meant "person of the wilderness" and they were said to have been elemental spirits of the woods. In some traditions, and again in an echo of the fairy tales of the Old World, pukwudgies had a sweet aroma and were often associated with flowers. Their magical powers included the ability to become invisible, to confuse human minds or to transform into cougars or other dangerous animals. In yet another similarity to fairy beliefs, they could cause harm to human beings merely by staring at them – echoing the European belief of the "evil eye." Finally, the name pukwudgie itself sounds vaguely familiar, at least to those who know William Shakespeare's comedy *A Midsummer Night's Dream,* in which, famously, the fairy is known as Puck, a name that has its origins in the puca, a Celtic entity or ghost that could be a bringer of both good and bad fortune.

Are all these similarities pure coincidence? Why do people from places as disparate as Ireland, Greece and New Zealand have beliefs in magical "little people?" What is it about the human race that leads to a nearly universal belief in diminutive beings who play tricks on people and sometimes cause them harm? Even the Far East, particularly Japan, has such tales. If a legend or belief in such creatures is so widespread, could it have a basis in fact?

I ask this question because I saw something I couldn't explain, again on my grandparents' property, when I was around 20 years old. I was out walking in the "back forty," an area of the property which is open field bordering on the woods, one fine sunny spring or summer day when I happened to see this rather slight fellow – much shorter than me - with his back to me, digging with a small spade or shovel at the edge of the forest. It was highly unusual to see strangers on our property, and I certainly didn't recognize this individual. The truly odd thing about him was that he was dressed entirely in green – olive green shirt, olive green pants, olive green hat – and he was shoveling slowly but intently, as though he were looking for something important buried in the ground. There was something unnerving about his presence.

I called out to the man, and he simply ignored me. I couldn't believe he didn't hear me, as I called out to him several times, saying something like, "Hello! What are you doing? This is private property!" He continued to act as if he hadn't heard me and went on digging as though he were searching for buried treasure.

I decided to go and get my grandmother, who was back at the house, and I told her about the man. She accompanied me out into the field, and she saw the man too, and was just as disturbed and mystified by his presence as I was. At that point, we both called out to the man, asking him what he was doing here, and at one point he turned as if to look at us. The creepy thing was that we couldn't see any features on his face, even though it was a bright, sunny afternoon. He was only a few yards from us, and we should have seen him clearly enough to recognize him, but when he turned to us, it was as though his face was a blank slate. Then he simply turned around again, his back to us, and continued with his digging as though we weren't even there.

Then we did something strange: we went back to the house. Sometimes, strange occurrences have that effect upon witnesses; it's as though the mind shuts down or shuts out what has just happened. We found ourselves sitting down at the dining room table. All these decades later, I still don't understand why we did that.

It was only a few minutes later that we realized what a strange thing that was for us to have done. We looked at each other, and the expressions on our faces said: Why did we come back to the house? It was quite disturbing to know that we couldn't explain our actions even to ourselves. We decided then and there to go into the back forty again and see if the man was still there.

When we trudged back to the field, we saw that the man was gone. In fact, not only was there no short, slight man in green, there was no evidence that anyone had been digging there at the edge of the woods. There was no disturbance of the soil. We had both been witness to the inexplicable.

This encounter was one of the strangest things that has ever happened to me. It's difficult to put into words how unsettling it was. I've often wondered who – or what – we saw that day. A small man dressed in green, digging as if for buried treasure? I've even entertained the thought that if I could just remember where he had been digging, would I find something valuable?

All of which brings us back to the little people. Our strange reaction to this encounter reminded me of what was once called "fairy glamour," a power that can make curious onlookers "unsee" what they have just witnessed. This ability was sometimes used to hide the whereabouts of a fairy, making it something of a magical survival skill.

The fairies of the distant past were far different from the modern-day "Tinkerbell" variety of fairies we're used to seeing in children's books and cartoons. The creatures of ancient times were usually the size of children, but they were generally old and wizened in appearance, although they could also be young and beautiful, as they were sometimes referred to as "The Shining Ones." They lived deep underground, beneath antediluvian burial mounds or in caves, in magical realms where time passed in a different manner from our own, where they never aged or died and their lives seemed eternal.

The "Good People" also were obsessed with human reproduction, stealing newborn human babies right out of their cradles and taking them to Fairyland, exchanging them with fairy babies – or sometimes with old and ugly fairies. The intention was to increase and improve their stock, as, for whatever reason, fairy births were often blighted with miscarriages and deformities. As such, they would attempt to strengthen their breed with new blood: ours.

There are numerous old Celtic tales of men becoming "bewitched" by fairies, and who would then find themselves having sexual relations with beautiful female fairies – and very often with the Fairy Queen herself, said to be "more beautiful than any woman on earth."

As was the case with the fictional Rip Van Winkle, "missing time" was also a feature of fairy abductions. Just as with Washington Irving's famous character, those who returned from the realm of the fairies usually found that days, weeks or even years had passed in what, to them, had felt like mere hours. Here's something disturbing about my own sighting of a strange little man digging by the woods: although Gram and I found ourselves back at the house shortly after seeing the man, we had no recollection of *walking* back to the house. We were just suddenly there. I truly can't account for that!

Now to postulate something even stranger: as numerous UFO researchers from the French scientist Jacques Vallee (basis for the character played by Francois Truffaut in *Close Encounters of the Third Kind*) to British writer Nick Redfern have observed, the similarities between fairies and aliens are extraordinary and impossible to overlook. And that leads us directly to the subject of our next chapter...

Chapter Four

UFOs in the Hudson Valley

When one gets reports from scientists, engineers and technicians whose credibility by all common standards is high and whose moral caliber seems to preclude a hoax, one can do no less than hear them out, in all seriousness. – J. Allen Hynek, UFO researcher and scientist

December 31st, 1981: A retired policeman – who preferred to remain anonymous – and his family saw a "boomerang-shaped object" drift slowly and almost silently over the top of their home in Kent, New York, a small town in the Hudson Valley. The witnesses could see a solid structure with as many as fifteen green, red and white lights attached to the object. It maintained a constant altitude at (an educated guess) around 150 meters, moved at a slow but steady pace, and emitted only a faint hum. Suddenly, the lights went out and three bright – nearly blinding – white lights in the shape of a triangle popped on in their place. Roughly five seconds later, the colored lights returned, and the object drifted out of sight.

Edwin Hansen, 55, was driving down nearby Interstate 84, just moments after the anonymous family's sighting, when he saw an object that he couldn't explain. Hansen and several other motorists pulled off to the side of the road to observe a boomerang-shaped formation of lights that projected a bright beam of light onto the ground. The object was so enormous that it blotted out most of the sky in front of Hansen, he later reported, and it made circles in the air, slowly revolving. At the second he thought he'd like to get a closer look at this anomaly, the object moved in his direction. He started to become afraid, but a voice in his head told him there was nothing to fear. At that same moment, the object turned away, and the beam went out. Hansen said that he had felt "thoughts that weren't his own" in his head and postulated that the UFO – or the occupants within – had communicated with him telepathically.

This was the beginning of the biggest UFO flap in the history of the Hudson Valley. The object that was variously referred to as 'The Triangle," "The Westchester Wing" or "The Westchester Boomerang" was eventually seen by over 7,000 witnesses, many of them doctors, lawyers, police officers and scientists. Most of the subsequent Hudson Valley UFO sightings indicated that the craft was a V-shaped fuselage with multi-colored lights all around it.

The sightings had a remarkably consistent pattern: the object was always seen at night, never in the daytime; the lights on the UFO changed color; when over a body of water, such as the Hudson River, the craft was seen displaying a beam of red light as if scanning the water's surface; and the object seemed to show a keen interest in the Indian Point Nuclear Power Plant – now known as the Indian Point Energy Center - in Westchester County, New York as though gathering information from it.

Kent, New York, where the object was first seen, is only about an hour's drive from Kinderhook down the Taconic Parkway. The UFO flap of the early to mid-1980s in the Hudson Valley remains one of the best-documented series of unidentified flying object sightings in history. The object was videotaped several times, investigated by the likes of famed UFO researcher J. Allen Hynek and researched by local and national journalists and law enforcement agencies, with the result that the sightings were never adequately explained.

Attempts at so-called "rational" explanations came up empty. Debunkers came up with "explanations" as varied as planes, balloons, the planet Venus and satellites, but they all turned out to be weak rationalizations that easily debunked themselves. Some debunkers sought to explain the sightings away as those of a blimp, but when contacted, blimp manufacturers and pilots all confirmed that no blimp had been in the area at the various times of the sightings.

After the initial reports, the sightings continued a couple of months later, in February 1982, when Monique O' Driscoll and her daughter drove down a country road to follow a lighted object in the sky. They observed it passing over their car. When it stopped to hover over a lake that had been frozen over, Monique exited her car to see it better. She later reported that the object had over 50 blue, red and amber lights, with a larger amber light in the middle of it. She described it as 60 to 90 meters across, its underside lined with metal supports and beams, rather like the underside of a bridge. The UFO began to turn away, but at the exact moment O'Driscoll wished for it to stay, it turned around and glided in her direction. When she became afraid, it turned back again and flew away. There were other witnesses who saw the object at the same time as O'Driscoll, as well as later that evening when it passed over I-84. The police in Carmel, Kent and across the state line in Danbury, Connecticut were swamped with phone calls reporting the UFO that night.

In the early Spring of 1983, the sightings continued when a woman in Brewster saw a V-shaped object with multiple lights "all the colors of the rainbow." There was one large light in the center, she reported, and the UFO then made a sharp turn and floated two doors down to pass over the home of Dennis Sant, the Deputy Clerk for Putnam County. Sant said that he had seen the object hovering over his home earlier that evening and had had an "urge" to go out and get a better look at it. He located it over I-84; he then ran back inside to get his family to come out and see it with him. He reported that the second he wished he could get a closer look, the object rotated in his direction. According to Sant, it had numerous green, red and white lights along its sides and an amber light that swept back and forth from one end of the "V" to the other. As it hovered above them, the lights seemed to grow to be three times as bright as they had been. Sant and his father were so close to it that he said they could see the craft's dark metallic surface and could hear what they thought was "a finely tuned engine sound."

On March 24th – the following week – more sightings occurred in Yorktown, this time with several police officers as witnesses. Their switchboards had been flooded with reports of a boomerang-shaped UFO that had green, blue and red lights. In nearby New Castle, an object "as large as a football field" was reported to police in that community, while meteorologist Bill Hele reported a V-shaped UFO that had six or seven lights and was roughly 400 meters long, which descended from around 600 meters to 300 or so and slowed in velocity as it got closer. Hele noticed that the lights all changed colors at various times as though they were on a rotating prism within the object. All at once, he reported, the lights went out, and the object was left in total darkness – or it vanished. The lights came back on between 30 and 40 seconds later and then the UFO turned to the north and flew away, with all the lights changing to green. At roughly the same time, witnesses in Putnam County – about 15 miles to the north – saw what they described as a smaller object that behaved in a similar manner. The press got hold of these sightings and it became something of a *cause celebre.*

The Westchester Rockland Daily newspaper published a story on the sightings along with some other local newspapers, and that night, the object came back. This was enough to bring in noted UFO researcher Philip J. Imbrogno, who began collecting eyewitness statements with the help of former Project Blue Book consultant J. Allen Hynek. Investigators from Hynek's Center for UFO Studies also joined in the investigation, amassing over 300 phone calls, many of which were released to the local press. The team estimated that there were several thousand witnesses to the anomalous event on the night of March 24th, nearly all of them contained in the areas in and around Westchester and Putnam counties, along the Taconic Parkway.

All the reports involved a boomerang or V-shaped object, and many of the reports involved the UFO hovering over a body of water. The behavior of the object tended to change, depending on the witnesses. Some reported seeing the lights jump from one area of the sky to another, disappearing and reappearing, and sometimes ejecting smaller, self-propelled UFOs.

A photo by the author of part of the glowing ring he found during the UFO-plagued summer of 1983.

While all this was going on in that wild year of 1983, I had an interesting experience of my own. One summer evening as I was out taking a stroll (as I am wont to do), I happened to notice something just off McCagg Road. There's a little side road – just a short hop, skip and a jump from my grandparents' home – that curves around for a few hundred feet before it rejoins McCagg. In that little turn-off, I saw something glowing. Upon approaching it, I saw that it was a perfect circle, probably 15 or so feet in diameter. There was no moon that night, but it was glowing in the starlight.

I'm aware, of course, that so-called "fairy rings" are usually just naturally occurring rings or arcs of mushrooms. One finds them ordinarily in forested areas, although they can sometimes be spotted in open fields in dark green grass or, conversely, in dead grass. This ring, however, was in the middle of the turn-off, glowing to beat the band on gravel, with no grass anywhere in sight.

There was something very peculiar about this "fairy ring," so I went back to the house – which was literally a minute or so away – got my camera and came back to take a photograph of the ring. I didn't use a flash because I wanted the glow to be plain in the picture. And it is. In retrospect, I wish I had stood back further from the ring, as, when the photo was developed, I was a bit disappointed to see that I didn't get the entire circle in the picture. What's there, however, remains interesting and certainly shows that the ring, whatever it was, glowed of its own power.

Now whether this had anything to do with the myriad UFO reports of that time, I have no idea. I merely offer it as an interesting sidenote to the bizarre goings-on of that wild year.

The night of October 26th, 1983, was another busy one in the Hudson Valley. Several witnesses reported seeing a formation of seven white lights flying overhead. The central light remained in one spot, but the other lights jumped around erratically, then came together in a cluster and flew off as one light. Some witnesses claimed they saw a small red "probe" detach itself from the object.

Two nights later, on October 28th, biomedical engineer Jim Brooke saw an enormous boomerang-shaped object covered with lights hover over the Croton Falls Reservoir. According to Brooke, it was at least 30 meters long and had nine red lights along its sides. He said it started to move around the area of the reservoir, staying at a consistent altitude of roughly four and a half meters above the level of the water. Brooke said that the UFO was completely silent, and that its lights went out every time a car passed by.

Ultimately, the Yorktown police department came up with a thin rationalization that the UFO was nothing more than a group of planes flying in formation. They were unable to verify that claim, however. Needless to say, light planes are buffeted about by the wind, and they make a lot of noise as well, which didn't deter the Putnam police from making a similar statement.

The debunking continued, but that didn't prevent a second wave of sightings that began on March 25th, 1984, almost exactly a year since the previous flap. This time, the shapes and sizes of the unidentified objects were more varied, and there were reports of crosses in the sky, flying X's and round objects, one of the latter of which was captured on video. Several witnesses reported objects that bathed them in beams of light. The night of March 25th, over 200 people reported UFOs over the Taconic Parkway; witnesses included the town police of Carmel. Nelson Macedo, the police chief of Danbury, Connecticut, was fishing from a boat on Candlewood Lake with several other people when he and his friends and family saw a saucer-shaped object hovering overhead that seemed to be covered in rotating lights. When the boat's lights were turned off, the object's lights went off too.

The Westchester Wing may have made an appearance much closer to Kinderhook in June of 1984, in the nearby town of Red Hook. The Columbia County newspaper the Register-Star had a story about it in its June 22nd edition, headlined, "V-Shaped Object Seen Flying Toward River." The article went on to reveal:

RED HOOK – About 10:30 AM on Thursday, Keith McGilvray, 15, of Metzger Road looked towards the sky and saw an 80-foot V-shaped object flying over his house in the direction of the Hudson River.

He said the UFO had a half dozen white lights on each side with a red light at the end.

After traveling to the river, the object came back towards the house and hovered over it without moving for a few minutes, said Keith and his father, who also saw the UFO. Both said the object began to shine lights on the ground when it was near the river. It eventually went southwest and disappeared.

The McGilvrays said several of their neighbors saw it, as did a few state troopers.

Trooper Fenn of the state police in Rhinebeck said he saw something that looked to him like several planes flying in formation in the direction of Albany at that time.

McGilvray said that when the UFO stopped in mid-air, it sounded like a diesel engine humming.

Blanche Coons of North Broadway here said she saw something that looked like cargo planes in formation, but they were going too slow and flying too low. It went in the direction of the Skypark, she said.

Troopers said they will investigate the sighting.

Back in Brewster, New York, Bob Pozzuoli captured an object on video on the night of July 24th. It looks very much like what everyone was describing.

One of the more unsettling reports occurred in June, when guards at the Indian Point Nuclear Plant saw an object hovering over the site, and reported that the plant's security systems shut themselves down during the sightings. Imbrogno and his team continued to investigate, although the sightings died down somewhat; nevertheless, the team managed to have a sighting of their own on March 21st, 1985, when they saw a round object bathed in lights suspended over a building. They saw it turn sharply in the sky and chased it down the interstate, to no avail.

All these sightings – and many more – are contained in the book *Night Siege* by Hynek, Imbrogno and journalist Bob Pratt. Published in 1987, the book was a posthumous publication for Hynek, who sadly had passed away the previous year. It's an extraordinarily valuable book to UFO researchers, covering some of the best-documented UFO incidents in history, with some data even corroborated on radar. There were some credible reports of missing time and so-called "alien abductions." Hynek noted the incidents of what is called "high strangeness" common to UFO reports all over the world, a term defined as "a quality of being peculiar, bizarre, utterly absurd."

On March 5th, 1985, UFO sightings were back in the news at the Hudson *Register-Star,* with the latest edition containing the headline, "Residents Challenge UFO Helicopter Theory." It seemed that the "airplanes in formation" theory had given way to "helicopters in formation..." or a blimp...or pilots playing a prank... take your pick. The article noted:

> CLAVERACK – A Claverack man who spent 15 "eerie" minutes observing an alleged UFO Thursday night says he is convinced that police theories that the craft was a helicopter are false.

"I know what I saw," said Ted Filli, owner of the Claverack Food Mart. "I know what airplanes and helicopters look like and it wasn't either of those."

"It was like a damn nightmare," he said with a laugh.

Mr. Filli said it was around nine Thursday night when the phone rang at his family's Brookbound Lane Road home.

It was his sister and brother-in-law, Mr. and Mrs. Erik Demski of Claverack, phoning from their Claverack Package Store to report a strange object in the sky they had seen while on Route 23 out of Hudson.

Mr. Filli, his wife Jacqueline and son Ted, 18, went outside to investigate. Mr. Filli grabbed a pair of binoculars.

There it was, a cigar-shaped object hovering stationary for as long as three or four minutes at some points, he said.

"The thing that sticks out in my mind are the windows...square windows," he recalled. "It was shaped like a cigar, but I couldn't actually see where it began and where it ended."

The family also observed some red lights on the craft and heard a low hum, he said.

Mr. Filli said that when a small airplane passed, the object dipped down and arose again when the airplane was gone.

At no point, he said, did the craft move at any great speed. "It just moseyed along."

Michael Price, of Blue Hill Road, Germantown, bets the UFO was a blimp.

"I was at home Thursday about 7:30 – 8 PM when there was a knock at the door. Standing there was Phil Leonard, a produce manager for IGA in Red Hook. He told me to come outside because there was a UFO over my house," Mr. Price said.

They both looked at it for a while and Mr. Price concluded it was a blimp from its shape and the way it was moving.

"I've seen blimps before. This looked like one. It had a droning type of motor. It definitely wasn't a bunch of helicopters. I could see a pilot control station on the bottom of the blimp. It had red lights."

He said the object was about 500 feet down the road and traveling low. He suggests someone get in touch with the Goodyear company to see if a blimp was in the area.

Mr. Price added, "There was an auto show in Connecticut last week. Maybe the blimp was involved with it."

However, Red Hook attorney Woody Klose said he tracked the object for about an hour and didn't hear any engines. He said he has flown planes, and this was not any type of aircraft with which he was familiar.

For about five minutes Thursday night, Ralph Bertelle tracked the object at Columbia-Greene Community College where he had just finished teaching a math course.

On his way to his car in the parking lot, he said he "saw six lights kind of off in the distance" coming from the south. "They were pretty bright, and they made me stop and look."

"At first, I thought it was from a mountain or hill in the distance, but when I got to my car, I realized they were moving.

"As I stayed there awhile, they came right toward the college and flew right overhead," he related.

He said he thought it was a formation of small planes, and the lights could have been navigation lights, but he was not sure.

"There were five in kind of an asymmetrical V-shape and one was in the back." He also mentioned that there were some red lights in addition to the bright white lights.

"I did hear a humming noise, which I thought was kind of like an engine noise," but he couldn't see the outline of a plane.

As the lights continued on, they were hidden from view, so Mr. Bertelle began driving to his Greene County home. Approaching the nearby Rip Van Winkle Bridge, he said he observed the same set of lights again, except they were going back from where they came.

He said the lights stayed "perfectly together in the same formation," flying at a constant speed at an unusually low altitude.

Despite these oddities, Mr. Bertelle expressed skepticism that what he witnessed was a visitor from space. He recalled an article he read in *Discover* Magazine a few months back, which indicated that unusual sightings in the Hudson Valley might be pilots playing a prank.

What was it then, that was in the skies over Columbia County that night in March 1985? Was it a helicopter, a blimp, a group of pilots playing a prank…or something else? At this late date, we'll probably never know, but as far as I'm aware, no one came forth to positively identify it as any of those things.

In September of that year, did a UFO crash in Columbia County? It seems that *something* did, as the *Register-Star* reported on September 11th:

Woman tells of Sparking, Glowing Object in Sky

STUYVESANT FALLS – The report of an explosion Monday night wasn't entirely unfounded, as authorities are treating it, according to a Stuyvesant Falls woman.

She asked that her name not be used lest "people think I'm losing my mind."

As she tells it, she was watching television and doing a puzzle between ten and eleven PM Monday when she saw a flash and heard a blast she took to be lightning and thunder. There was also a second blast, with no flash, so she unplugged her TV and found her kitchen hall lit up, though her lights were not on.

She said she looked outside and saw a glowing orange body, resembling a streetlight, hanging in the air in the area of Route 23 and Route 9H giving off sparks or balls like a Roman candle for one and a half to two minutes. She said whatever it was was higher than the telephone lines but low enough that a neighbor on the other side of the woods could not see it because of the trees.

The woman also said she could see a smoke trail from the bottom of the bulb, as if it had risen from the ground.

She quoted the neighbor as saying, he, too, heard the two explosions and had gone to look in the area but saw nobody around. She quoted him as saying he smelled gunpowder but thought it might have been the power of suggestion.

She said she did not think what she saw was the common schoolboy prank of burning something inside a plastic bag so that the glowing fumes create a balloon and the effect of a homemade 'UFO.'

"It was the weirdest thing I ever saw," she said.

According to Columbia County Fire Control, Stockport firefighters responded to an unfounded report of a small explosion and fire near the Hudson River at 10:21 PM Monday.

Police in Coxsackie, Greene County, reported what appeared to be a fire on the east bank of the river. A check of the area produced no results.

This event occurred no more than eight miles from my grandparents' house. When I read about it, I went down to the area near the intersection of Route 23 and Route 9H – a location I knew very well – and couldn't find any evidence of an explosion, or any wreckage of an object. But that doesn't negate the eyewitness reports, and there were more in the September 19th edition of the *Register-Star:*

Sept. 9 'Plane Crash' Reports Still Linger

WEST GHENT – Area residents are coming forward with more details of what authorities chalked up as an "unfounded report" of an explosion at 10:21 PM on September 9th in the West Ghent-Stockport area.

Barbara McCagg of County Route 22 said she is convinced she saw a plane crash despite reports from area airports that no planes were missing.

A check with police, who sometimes fly helicopters in the area, revealed they had no aircraft there at the time either.

Mrs. McCagg said she was standing at her front door at the time of the incident and saw something that appeared to be on fire tumbling through the sky. When the object appeared to pull into a glide, she recognized what she said were airplane lights.

Mrs. McCagg said she thought a plane might be on landing approach at nearby Columbia County airport, a common sight at her home. But the lights dipped below the tree line and went out, she said.

A tremendous white flash, like an explosion, followed and rose above the trees for a distinct line – like a pencil line across the sky. Because her television was playing, she heard no explosion, she said.

Mrs. McCagg also thought something may have hit the power lines running through the area, but she experienced no power problems.

Richard Schumacher, district manager of Niagara-Mohawk Power Corp., said no power outages were reported in the area.

Mrs. McCagg said she has been unable to sleep nights, wondering whether someone was lying killed or injured in the wooded and swampy area between her home and County Route 25. She said the woods would obstruct the view of anyone looking for the wreckage from the road, as firefighters did.

"I really believe I saw an airplane crash that night," she said, adding that she does not believe pranksters were behind the incident.

She also said an acquaintance, John Knitt, of Knitt Road in Stockport, heard two "cracks" that night and found a large tree limb had broken off the same time as the incident.

Mr. Knitt said he was awakened by two cracks, which sounded like someone pounding at his door, at about 10:30 PM on September 9th. He later found a maple tree limb, two feet in diameter, had broken from a tree in his yard.

Mr. Knitt said he saw no activity in the area that night and found no debris besides the limb.

Mrs. McCagg and Mr. Knitt said they wondered whether a plane may have been on an illegal drug run, which would explain the lack of report of any missing plane.

Coxsackie police started the official check of the incident when they reported what appeared to be an explosion and fire on the east bank of the Hudson River.

A Stuyvesant Falls woman reported the day after the incident seeing a glowing, bulb-like object hanging in the air and spitting sparks.

Gary Levine, professor of social science at Columbia-Green Community College, has spent time checking on reports of this and other similar sightings.

He said a similar sighting was reported in Greenville in February.

"The best way to record such an event is to photograph it," he said.

"'Unless someone gets a picture, there's nothing to go on,' he said."

We're left with a real mystery here. Several witnesses plus an entire police department reported explosions and a fire on that September night. At least one woman saw a "glowing orange ball" that emitted sparks. Yet no downed plane was ever found, nor was any other debris.

I think we can rule out any "drug-running" planes, as two of the witnesses speculated. There's absolutely no evidence for it, as there was – apparently – no plane involved.

Could it have been a meteorite? I think we can rule that out too, as at least one of the witnesses said it moved upward. It has some of the hallmarks of a meteorite crash: glowing orange, leaving a smoke trail, etc. A meteorite, however, never moves *upward.* Nor can it "hang there" in the sky. So, if that witness can be believed, we can rule out a meteorite as well.

Could it have been a prank? It seems doubtful, as the fire it caused was large enough to be noticed by the Coxsackie police, who are based across the river in Greene County. If it was a prank, it was certainly an elaborate one, and there has never been anyone either suspected of pulling a prank or of anyone who came forward to admit it.

What we're left with is an anomaly. Something apparently crashed in Columbia County that September night in 1985, but we may never know what it was. Meanwhile, we can only speculate regarding the object the witnesses saw. It remains "unknown."

Your humble author came that close – *that close* – to seeing the Westchester Wing in 1996, when I was riding back to Albany, New York with some friends from a convention in New Jersey. We were on the New York State Thruway – site of hundreds of UFO reports – and it was around 9PM, when Susan, the woman in the group, who was sitting in the front seat with her husband Colin– who was driving – suddenly became animated and shouted, "What was that, what was that, what was *that?*"

I was sitting in the back seat with a fellow named Tony, and we immediately looked out the car windows at the darkened road, where we were expecting to see an accident. Unfortunately, we missed what Susan and her husband had seen in the sky: a V-shaped object that sounded like a perfect description of the Westchester Wing. By the time we looked up, the object was gone. In other words, we two backseat passengers were a day late and a dollar short.

Fortunately, Susan is a talented artist and sometime later she drew the object she had seen, along with writing an account of what had occurred. She wrote: "A year ago, in April 1996, Colin and I 'saw something.' He was driving and I was in the passenger seat when a slow moving, large triangular object moved silently over our car and kept going off into the dark, rainy night. Its surface appeared to be a dull brushed metal, yet it was almost self-illuminated, without glowing, and without lights.

"Our two backseat passengers saw nothing.

"One is a UFO researcher in his spare time."

Is my face red? Once again, the "monster hunter" – or in this case the UFO hunter – never gets to see his quarry. Although there *was* one time…but I'll get to that later.

For this book, I interviewed my friend Susan about her sighting. This is the transcript of that conversation, in which I refer to Susan as "SL:"

BGH: What you saw didn't make any sound, did it?

SL: That's correct. We were driving on the New York Thruway. I think we were about an hour outside the city, in the Poughkeepsie area, I think. I could see the lights from cars that were passing; you know how you can see them reflected on the inside of your car windows? I was kind of watching those, and then I realized that one of them was not behaving like that. It was just continuing in the same direction. I looked up and I could see that something was coming over the car, so I pulled the window down and I was like, "Whoa!" Both Colin and I were like, "What was that?"

BGH: I remember you saying three times, "What was that, what was that, what was *that?*" And I looked at the road; I thought there was an accident or something.

SL: Yeah, of course, it was more likely that there was a dead deer in the road than a visitor from beyond or something!

BGH: Everybody said that it made no sound, and that's actually very typical of UFOs in general; they're just silent.

SL: I've seen other things before, when I was a kid. I've always been obsessed with science fiction and fantasy and stuff like that. I remember a few times when I would say, "That's a UFO!" And my dad would say, "No, that's a helicopter light." He was in the Army, and he would say, "That's just the light on a helicopter." But this was different. And Colin saw it too.

BGH: What do you think the Westchester Wing was? Do you have any theories on that?

SL: I don't know. Some people said it was the Stealth Fighter. But it was not going very fast, maybe 40 miles an hour, I would say. I rolled down the window to stick my head out and look up at it. You know how stainless steel can have kind of a brushed look to it? It looked like that, a dark gun-metal grey and it seemed like it was illuminated, but it was solid. I don't know of anything that looks like that, except something molten or ashes glowing from within. Nothing else really looks like that, so I'm having a hard time finding an analogy. We both saw the same thing, and when we got home, I asked Colin to draw it, and I drew it too, separately, to make sure we weren't influencing each other, and we both drew the same thing. It looked like a guitar pick, that shape. But as if the guitar pick was inflatable!

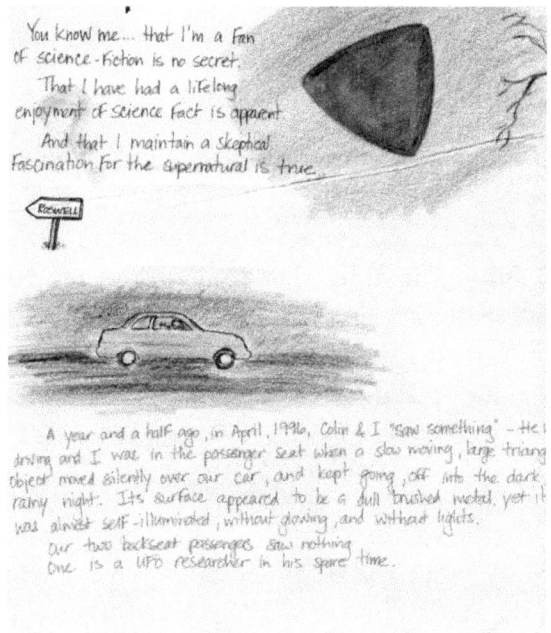

Drawing made by Susan L. of her UFO sighting over the New York Thruway.

61

BGH: Yeah, it's been described as triangular or boomerang-shaped, but basically the same kind of shape.

SL: Some described it as having a jagged edge in the back, but that's not what I saw. It was an equilateral triangle. That's what I remember and that's what I drew when I got home. I can't find that original drawing; it may just have been on a piece of scrap paper and maybe that's why I re-drew it a year later, which is the drawing you have.

BGH: I keep kicking myself, years later, for missing that!

SL: Well, why would you think that I saw something like that? It's not like I said, "Oh my God, it's an alien!" Honestly, it was so... "Did you see that? Did you see that?" I was so glad that Colin also saw it, or I would just have been, like, in doubt.

BGH: I know a lot of people at the time were saying, "Well, it must be the Stealth Bomber." There are several problems with that theory. Number one: even though it was "stealthy," the Stealth Bomber still made a lot of noise.

SL: Oh, yeah! There was no noise. I presumed it to be the height of the trees. The trees were, say, 30 feet tall or something. It was just over that level. And it was slow. Any airplane is not going to go that slow or that low, no matter what it is. It doesn't have that capability. There was no sound I could hear. It was raining so I suppose if there was any sound, it would have been drowned out by the water and the wind.

Author/artist Lisa LaMonica also saw the Westchester Wing, or something very much like it, circa 1982. She told me, "We were in a plaza, like one of the plazas in Hudson, and it was very low, it was silent. We looked around and couldn't understand why more people weren't aware of it, I think because there were so many lights around anyway; but it was V-shaped. But I didn't know about the Westchester

Wing until I moved up here, and it started to be more talked about on TV; up to that point, it wasn't something I'd heard much about. But in the Hudson Valley, it was a big deal for many years. It's got to be related to nuclear power stations in the area, perhaps. Maybe that's why these objects were around."

The Westchester Wing was hardly the first UFO to be reported in the Hudson Valley. The region's spooky reputation was partly founded on the fact that weird lights have been seen in and on the Hudson River since the 1700s. According to Ellenville, New York historian Richard McPhillips, "In the 1700s, these sailors were going up and down the Hudson River from New York City to…Albany and, at night, they would see these unusual lights on both sides of the river. They were very afraid. A lot of the sailors were kept in line because, if they screwed up, the threat was that they were going to throw them over to land, and they'd have to deal with these lights at night."

According to UFO researcher Linda Zimmerman, UFOs were documented in the Hudson Valley as far back as 1909. Contemporary news reports referred to an "airship" that flew only at night and was seen moving along the Hudson River from town to town.

In 1953, a boy named Hank Vanderbeck was playing with some friends in Saugerties when he saw a cigar-shaped object, tapered at each end, with hoops of alternating green and white lights that encircled the roughly 300-foot-long craft. The object hovered over Saugerties for some 20 minutes, causing such a sensation that fighter jets from the nearby Stewart Air Force base were dispatched, but couldn't close in on the object, which moved away and out of sight at amazing speed.

Circa 1965, my Uncle George was putting a new back door on my grandparents' house, and he didn't finish the job until after dark. I was out on the porch with him as we both happened to look up into the starry night sky to see an object far, far up that was not a plane. It was just a pinpoint of light, but it was moving fast. Whether it was a UFO or perhaps a satellite, we couldn't say for sure. But we watched the white object as it crossed from one horizon to the other.

A few years later, in the late 1960s or early 1970s, a relative of mine was driving through the town of Castleton on Route 9J, a country road that runs parallel to the Hudson River, when he saw, off the road in a nearby field, a very strange object. He claimed at the time that it was "diamond-shaped," had red and blue lights and was hovering not far off the ground. Feeling rather uneasy, he didn't waste any time getting out of there. Years later, when I asked him about it, he denied ever having seen it, but I suspect that his conservative nature – and the fact that he knew I wrote books about such things, and he didn't want to be quoted – made him retract his statement. This person is now deceased, but I'm still withholding his name out of respect.

In 1968, a Crawford, New York resident named Harold Hunt was crossing Red Mills Bridge when he saw a "metallic object" that he said measured 70 to 100 feet in diameter, which bathed his car in light. Hunt was, shall we say, uneasy as the object followed him for a short time before it vanished into the night sky.

Speaking of Crawford, Officer Robert Comeau of that town's police department had his own sighting in 1971 when he was awakened out of a sound sleep by a whirring noise from outside. Looking out his window at the star-strewn sky, Comeau saw a silver disc-shaped craft hovering several feet from his house. Comeau watched the object for some 40 minutes – but apparently never thought to take a picture of it.

Right next to the Town of Crawford is Pine Bush, a hamlet in Orange County that's about an hour and 45-minute drive from Kinderhook. Pine Bush has been known as "The UFO Capital of New York" since the 1990s, despite being – on the surface at least – a typical suburban town. In his book *Weird New York,* author Chris Gethard notes, "The Hudson Valley of New York has long been home to some truly weird occurrences… most famously, the Hudson Valley has been known to attract strange vessels and beings from outer space. Pine Bush has come to be known worldwide as the primary destination for these extraterrestrial visitors to the area."

Although many residents of Pine Bush started reporting sightings dating back to the 1960s, it wasn't until the 1990s that the town's reputation as the UFO capital of New York – if not of the entire east coast – was secured due to some high-profile sightings that were a sort of byproduct of the Westchester Wing sightings. During that unusually long UFO flap, several witnesses reported having contact with extraterrestrial beings; in fact, over 60 people claimed to have been abducted by bizarre alien creatures, with young women between the ages of 25 and 30 – it should be noted, peak child-bearing ages – representing many so-called abduction cases.

While the Westchester Wing was flying around the Hudson Valley and startling its residents through several counties, incidents that were just as strange – if not even stranger – were taking place in Pine Bush. As Gethard pointed out in his book, "As the hype over the Westchester sightings died down, more and more people began to realize that truly strange, phenomenal things were occurring in the seemingly normal rural village."

Many residents of Pine Bush began reporting objects that were emphatically different from the Westchester Wing in the mid to late 1980s. With alarming frequency, they reported seeing "pencil-thin" hovering crafts, balls of orange or white light, and other types of objects along with the Westchester craft itself. There were also reports of "strange strobe lights" seen in the woods just outside the village, along with reports of strange sounds and sightings at the Jewish Cemetery on Route 52.

In 1991, author Ellen Crystall published her book *Silent Invasion: The Shocking Discoveries of a UFO Reporter.* Crystall, formerly of California, now resided in New Jersey and had been visiting Pine Bush for 11 years, documenting UFO encounters by interviewing the locals. Her book included controversial photos that were alleged to be of alien craft. When the media began to report on what was happening in Pine Bush after the publication of her book, journalists began to converge on the town.

When the citizens of Pine Bush began to share their strange stories with each other, they came to realize just how many – and how varied – they were. Some told of groups of a dozen or more UFOs soaring over the village, and by the middle of the 1990s, Pine Bush became recognized as one of the hottest of UFO hot spots.

Crowds of people began to gather nightly around the village, ultimately becoming known as "skywatchers" or "UFO-ers." The area they frequented most was at West Searesville Road, where hundreds of people reported seeing strange objects in the night sky. The gatherings became so large that the police were forced to ban the skywatchers from that area due to the fact they were disrupting traffic.

The "UFO-ers," however, were a grass-roots movement, and they could not be stopped that easily. Smaller groups still congregated at South Searesville and the Jewish Cemetery, where "unidentified animal sightings" were reported to have occurred. The *Times-Herald Record,* a local newspaper, reported a fascinating sighting by Pine Bush resident John Lewis, who videotaped - in broad daylight, no less - a "thin black object" overhead. From the article: "Lewis watched the object move slowly downward at a 45-degree angle for about five minutes… Then he rushed for his video camera. The unidentified flying object was pencil-shaped and black with a long tail. There was not a hint of reflection from the sun."

The *Poughkeepsie Journal* published a report by witness Bill Wiand concerning one of his encounters with "aliens." Wiand related, "I did recently have an invasion, and it terrified me… It started like it always does, with the noise in my ears and it just kind of rumbles through. I couldn't move my body, but I could move my eyes, and I knew the room was filled with entities." The article also pointed out that there had been other "abductions" in and around Pine Bush, including one involving an anonymous person who claimed, "They immobilized me and undressed me and put this device on my genitals and took a sperm sample."

The *Times-Herald* also featured a piece about the claims made by Pine Bush resident Jim Smith, a sergeant at Woodbourne

Correctional Facility, who reported, "I've seen so many of the beings, I know exactly how they move. They're different sizes, different shapes, but when you see them so much, you know they're not of this Earth."

Smith continued: "Not long ago, I saw this figure about six foot six and dressed in all black standing beneath the traffic light in Pine Bush… When she moved, it wasn't like walking. It wasn't in frames either, like most of them move. In frames, they're someplace and then they're suddenly in another place, like time-lapse photography. But this one moved horizontally.

"In Pine Bush," Smith went on, "you see things you don't expect. I've seen a cat with no head walking across the floor. It just had a piece of cardboard where the head should be. A lot of people in Pine Bush tell me they've seen that cat. But not everyone can see the cat or the beings. You have to be open to things like that."

Over the past thirty years and more, Pine Bush has been host to a lot of construction and suburban development, and the UFO stories have died down somewhat. Nevertheless, sightings of bizarre creatures and accounts of "high strangeness" have continued, including what Gethard refers to as "shadowy figures, strange noises permeating desolate areas, flashing lights and more."

During the past couple of years – and despite the pandemic – The Pine Bush UFO and Paranormal Museum has opened, which includes guided museum tours, gallery lectures by UFO researchers and other special events. There's even a "haunted" Halloween event called "The Crop Circle," an outdoor walk through a corn maze all during the month of October. The residents of Pine Bush have truly embraced their paranormal heritage and seek to share it with tourists.

Aside from the fictional Rip Van Winkle, the most famous case of abduction in the Catskills by "little people" belongs to novelist Whitley Streiber, who claimed that he was abducted from his cabin near Kingston, New York on the night after Christmas, 1985 by what he described as "non-human beings." Strieber, best known for his horror novels *Wolfen* and *The Hunger* (both of which were made into feature films) recounted his experiences with these beings in his non-fiction book, *Communion,* which was published in 1987.

Strieber never claimed the beings to be extraterrestrial. Although the book is generally accepted as a book about alien abduction, Strieber refers to the beings as "the visitors" to this day, a name he deliberately chose to remain as neutral as possible as to their origins. Since the publication of *Communion,* Strieber has written four additional non-fiction tomes about his ongoing experiences, in which he postulates that the human species is undergoing a transformation to a higher level of consciousness, guided by "the visitors," who may or may not be from another dimension or another time. He even postulates in one of his books that they may be our own dead, experiencing the afterlife right in front of our eyes.

Strieber has frequently expressed his frustration that his experiences have been taken to involve alien contact when he has never made such a claim himself. Strieber has also written about "paranormal" childhood experiences and suggested that he may have been the subject of these contacts for his entire life.

Needless to say, Strieber has encountered more than "the visitors": skepticism of his claims has been rampant, fueled by the fact that he was previously known as a writer of fantastic fiction, and that his imagination must have run away with him. I'm quite familiar with that sort of accusation myself, but it doesn't hold water. Authors know the difference between what they imagine and what is reality. At least, the good ones do.

Some have implied that Strieber suffered from some sort of brain abnormality, but he underwent tests for temporal lobe epilepsy - a condition that can cause hallucinations - at his own request and his brain was found to be functioning normally.

Whatever happened – and continues to happen – with Strieber, your respectful author finds it very interesting that these incidents allegedly occurred in the exact neck of the woods where Washington Irving wrote that Rip Van Winkle was "abducted" for his 20-year nap. Coincidence?

I have one personal anecdote regarding UFOs, and it is, I think, a good one. One fine evening in 1974 – just before my 22nd birthday – my grandmother and I gazed in wonder upon a dazzling light show in the sky that we could see from our dining room window which overlooked the Catskill Mountains. In the distance, seemingly over the Hudson River, were several reddish-orange balls of light that were flying about just as the sun was setting. They began as separate entities, as it were; four or five of them, doing seemingly impossible maneuvers such as 360-degree turns and then stopping on a dime, then hovering in the sky. At that point, they circled around again, and then – perhaps strangest of all – they all gathered in one big cluster, like one single entity, before separating again. We watched these bizarre objects, which certainly seemed to be intelligently controlled, for about ten minutes. I had a movie camera somewhere in the house, which I didn't even think to pick up. I was utterly absorbed, as was my grandmother, in what seemed to be a "show" put on for our benefit.

Finally, all the objects flew off in complete silence – as indeed the entire experience had been - splitting up into various points in the sky until they vanished out of sight.

I have never come up with a so-called "rational" explanation for this sighting. It remains the only time in my life that I believe I saw genuinely unexplained aerial phenomena. It's as vivid in my memory now as it was over 40 years ago, and I will never forget this brush with the vast, cosmic unknown.

Chapter Five

The Kinderhook Creature

Every single country has its version. Yeti, Yowie in Australia, Wild Man in China. So, I don't know if it's perhaps a myth that stems from the last of the Neanderthals. But then is this the last of the Neanderthals still living in these remote forests? I don't know. But I'm not going to say it doesn't exist and I'm not going to say that people who believe in it are stupid. – Primatologist Jane Goodall, 2021

In addition to everything else, Kinderhook also seems to be the home – or at least a gathering place – for a small (but vocal) group of bigfoot-type creatures which have often been sighted, heard and tracked. I'm one of those trackers; I've made plaster casts of both three and five-toed prints that are large and anomalous.

Several members of my family encountered these creatures in the early 1980s. The encounters ranged from finding tracks and hearing strange vocalizations to actual eyewitness reports of one or more of these creatures either seen in the woods or walking along the roads.

I had heard of "monsters" roaming the Hudson Valley as far back as the 1970s, and quite honestly, I was skeptical. It was all very well to have the yeti in the Himalayas and the sasquatch romping around the Pacific Northwest, but such creatures in my own back yard? The very idea seemed rather silly.

In 1978, however, I read an article in the now-defunct *Hudson River Chronicle* concerning sightings of hairy, bipedal anthropoids in nearby Dutchess County, and in such Columbia County towns as Canaan, Chatham and Nassau. It was late in that same year that unusual footprints were found near my grandparents' home and near my parents' home – the latter of which borders on a huge tract of swampland known only to the locals as Cushing's Hill.

The tracks found in my grandparents' woods were three-toed and very large indeed. My cousin Barry, who was only 13 at the time, was already an experienced trapper and hunter. In December 1978, he found the tracks in newly fallen snow in the woods; they were crossing a log. He showed them to me; I photographed them and sent the photos to the *Chronicle*. Unfortunately, the people who received them promptly lost them, along with the negatives (which I had foolishly sent also, so they would know I wasn't faking anything). This carelessness may explain why the magazine went out of business shortly afterwards!

As for the prints themselves, I was mystified by them. There were only three of them, and they seemed to end in the middle of an open space. Unless the creature somehow took flight, that seemed physically impossible.

It was around that same period of time that my grandmother looked out of her kitchen window early one morning, just as the sun was rising, and saw what was apparently some sort of large creature that was curled up and seemingly resting on the lawn. As dawn was just streaking the sky, she couldn't see it clearly, but it looked strange enough to her that she decided not to tell anyone about it, for fear of being called "strange" herself.

"I didn't tell anyone," she later said to me, "because I was afraid people would cart me away somewhere. It was only afterward, when other people said they had seen the same thing, that I talked about it."

Gram then proceeded to tell the story: "There was some big black thing all curled up down at the end of the lawn one morning when I got up really bright and early. And then I saw tracks (in the snow), and I never said a word because I thought they were going to say, 'She's nutty.'"

"I had my garbage in a green bag, the same as I have on the back porch now, only I had it up here by the corner of the house and it used to be (around this time) taken up and set down in the lawn down there (near where she saw the creature) and things were taken out of it."

"The bag wasn't torn," she continued. "But the food was taken out, and just as though a person took it out or something – nothing like an animal would do, and I kept wondering about that because if the dogs get in it… it's all over the place, and this wasn't. It was very neat."

"And my neighbor over here called me after that, and she said her garbage that she had in a shed had had the same thing done to it. And she… found the empty bag in a tree… it was just picked up out of the shed and carried away."

Gram was 72 years of age at that time and, understandably, she didn't want people to think she'd gone "funny in the head." It was only after others started reporting these things that she told me what the creature on the lawn had looked like: "I think it had quite long hair. And it was very tall. It was sort of circled, curled up."

The detail that it was "curled up" conjures up images of the Russian "alma," a so-called wild man that has been seen sleeping in that very position. The American sasquatch has also sometimes been described as sleeping in this semi-fetal position.

Gram continued relating her experience to me with even more bizarre details: "The one thing about that creature, whatever it is," she said, "it seems to appear and disappear. One minute it's there and the next minute it's gone. And we have seen tracks leading somewhere and even the tracks seem to stop right there, and you don't see them anymore. That's a mystery. The whole thing is a mystery to me."

Tracks that my father attributed to a bear were seen all that winter. He is also an experienced hunter and woodsman, and he found something while hunting in the heights of Cushing's Hill that year that could not have had anything to do with bears, however. He found three dead rabbits that were stuffed into the snow at the top of the hill, as though they were being stored away for the winter. The odd thing was that there were no tracks in the vicinity at all, minus his own, and it was in a very remote spot. Nor was there any blood around the rabbits.

The rest of that year – and into the spring of 1979 – was devoid of "creature" activity, at least as far as I've been able to ascertain. It was nearly a year later – on December 5, 1979, to be exact – that

The author's paternal grandmother, Martha Hallenbeck, standing where she saw the Kinderhook Creature in 1979.

things started switching into high gear around Kinderhook. The activity seemed to center around Cushing's Hill. This time, it wasn't just tracks that were seen.

Again, I will leave it to Gram to describe what happened: "My grandson Barry was setting traps one day (in the swamp near Cushing's Hill, roughly a mile from my grandparents' house) and he came back and his face was so white – as white as could be, and he said to me, 'Grandma, I saw four great big things crossing the creek and going into the woods down there.' And I'm sure he saw something because I hadn't mentioned anything I'd seen before that."

I was there with my grandmother that afternoon when my cousin came running into the house. He was indeed as white as a sheet and quite terrified. He had a baseball bat with him that he used to kill muskrats when he was trapping, and he felt that the bat was no match for the creatures he had seen. He also told us that the things had made strange grunting and "clacking" sounds. As Gram put it in her usual low-key, ironic way: "So he ran all the way home, and he didn't go trapping there again right away."

The creatures he had seen that afternoon, although partially concealed by the dense underbrush of the swamp, were, according to him, light brown furry creatures that walked from one side of the creek to the other, clacking and grunting as they went. He went on to say that they were big, bigger than he was; and even at age fourteen, he was a strapping boy of nearly six feet. He pointed out the most interesting detail of all: unlike bears, they were walking on two legs.

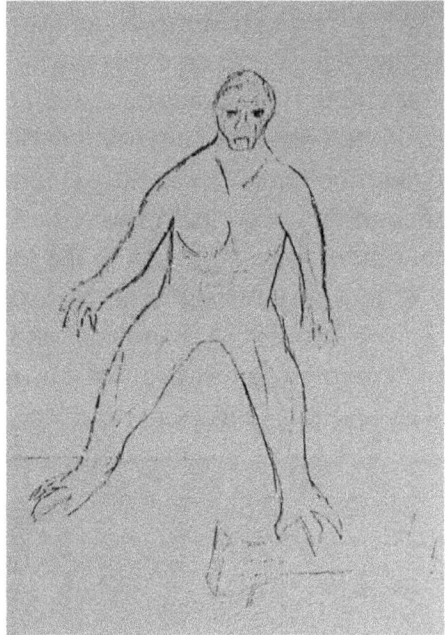

Drawing made by the author's cousin Barry of one of the creatures he saw near Cushing's Hill in late 1979.

After Barry reported his sighting, a friend and I decided to investigate the area. We couldn't get Barry to go back there, so we were joined by my other cousin, Russell. We didn't find any footprints; we crossed some fairly rough terrain, nearly got stuck in some sinkholes and discovered that a mere mile from my grandparents' home, the swamp near Cushing's Hill almost seemed to be another world.

In April 1980, one of the best sightings of all was reported by a woman who preferred to remain anonymous, but whose first name was Barbara. The woman was driving home from her job in Albany one evening on Route 9. She had just entered Columbia County; on her right were woods and, on her left, an unplanted cornfield.

Her car's headlights flashed on a creature that she described as being about seven and a half feet tall with reddish brown hair or fur. She was startled beyond belief at what she was seeing: "A highly evolved ape," as she told me. She slowed her car and watched in fascination as the creature walked across the road, ignoring her completely, and sauntered into the cornfield.

I didn't learn of this sighting until nearly a year later, when I interviewed the woman. She did not get out of her car during her sighting – and who could blame her? – so she never thought to look for tracks. One can only imagine the footprints in the spring mud, and I can't help but think of whoever owned the field scratching his or her head at the mysterious – and enormous – footprints in the cornfield.

The first time I personally heard the vocalization of what I believe to be the creature was on a July evening in 1980. A friend of mine was visiting from England. She and I were just leaving my grandparents' house to walk to where she was staying, as it was a beautiful full moon. At eleven o'clock, just as we walked out the door and onto my grandparents' porch, the security light went on, and at that moment we heard the most incredible sound emanating from the nearby woods, probably from the top of the hill. It was the powerful vocalization of some animal, starting off with a series of grunting noises, morphing into a crescendo of high-pitched shrieking or screaming and finally dying down in a low moan. It lasted for perhaps thirty seconds.

After a moment or two of stunned silence, my friend turned to me and said – with typical British understatement – "Is that a typical American sound to hear at night?"

"No!" I assured her, surprising myself with the intensity of my reply. "I've never heard that sound before in my life!"

At the time, I was still somewhat skeptical of the possibility of a bigfoot-type creature living, quite literally, in our neck of the woods, so I didn't press the issue to investigate the origin of the sound. Especially in the dark. Let's put it this way: it wasn't the type of sound you would want to run *toward.*

It was on the night of September 24th, 1980 – a night I'll never forget – that I became convinced there was something very strange in the woods. The whole day had been so odd, in fact, that I wrote about it in the diary that I kept that fateful year. That afternoon, I had taken a

75

walk around the golf course just up the road from my grandparents' house, and on the way back, I took the road that went past my parents' property, which was heavily wooded on both sides. I had the uncomfortable feeling that I was being watched – and followed. It seemed as though when I took a step, something in the forest on my right took a step, as if trying to keep pace with me. It was a very strange feeling, and one that I had never felt on that road before.

My diary entry read: "Incredible day. Walked around the golf course in the afternoon and had the weirdest sensation of being followed by something but could see nothing unusual."

Early that evening, my cousin Barry and I took a walk around that same golf course as the full moon – one of the biggest and brightest I'd ever seen – rose in the sky. We were both gently making fun of the whole bigfoot story as we walked. Even though my cousin had seen some very unusual creatures only a year or so before, he was trying to make himself believe that it had been something else – bears, deer, anything he could think of to rationalize his experience.

In my diary, I wrote of our walk: "Later, Barry and I walked around the golf course again and heard all the dogs barking their heads off." Perhaps they were barking at the full moon. Perhaps.

A detail of a drawing by the author's cousin, Barry, of one of the creatures he saw near Cushing's Hill in late 1979.

I finished my diary entry for that day by writing: "Went out to Chatham at about 9PM, was called by my grandmother who wanted me to come home because there was a 'something' outside the house terrifying her. By the time I got home, it was gone."

In fact, by the time I got home, I felt rather like the Richard Dreyfuss character in Steven Spielberg's *Close Encounters of the Third Kind,* walking around and saying, "This is nuts!" Barry was there with his shotgun, Gram was talking excitedly about what had happened, and my Aunt Barbara – Barry's mother – was in a state of semi-panic, a nervous wreck.

As it was told to me, what happened that evening while I was out was nothing less than an "invasion" of my grandparents' property by a creature or creatures unknown. Unfortunately, my grandfather was away on a camping trip, or he would have experienced it too. As it was told to me, my Aunt Barbara had brought Gram home from her house in the village late that evening. Also accompanying her were Barbara's daughter, Chari, and Chari's infant daughter, Melanie, who was just six months old. Aunt Barbara got out of her car with Gram to help her carry some water jugs onto the porch, when suddenly they heard some startling vocalizations from what seemed like only a few feet away.

"What in the world was that?" Gram exclaimed.

Barbara didn't answer her. She just stood there in what appeared to be a state of shock, frozen to the spot. The screams continued from around the corner of the old root cellar. Chari was still in the car with her baby. "Get back in the car, mom!" she shouted, as she heard the screams too. Then she proceeded, in panic, to lock all the car doors before her mother could get back inside!

Barbara didn't know what to do. She decided that maybe she'd better go home and get her son, Barry, who could bring his shotgun. Meanwhile, Chari realized her mistake and unlocked the car door so her mother could get inside. When Barbara finally managed to get into the car and speed away out of the driveway, Gram elected – for some reason that she couldn't even explain to me later – to stay home and protect the house. She was all alone there, and that's when she called me. She had armed herself with a hammer.

I must admit at this late date that I was skeptical when I first received that phone call. I was out with friends at a restaurant, and it was very unusual for Gram to call me in such a situation. I thought that maybe some animal was making noises outside the house. But when I stopped to think of it, Gram was not one to be afraid of any animals and she almost never called me when I was out with friends.

In fact, Gram was afraid of practically nothing; once, many years before, she had chased three hunters with guns off her property because they were trespassing! So, I came to the conclusion that something pretty strange was happening here. I finished a quick conversation with my friends and said goodbye to them.

Gram, meanwhile, told me later that while she was waiting for me, she sat in her chair in the living room watching all the windows, afraid of what might be peering in. She saw nothing, but she held her hammer while she looked around.

Gram later described those moments to me in detail: "When she (Barbara) backed out of the driveway, the thing went down below the hill and it just moaned – oh, the most terrible moan and groan – until the car lights were back in the driveway. Then it came right back up here again and made all those noises again, until he (Barry) got his gun."

When Barry arrived, he immediately heard the screams from just around the root cellar. He fired his shotgun into the air three times to scare off the intruder – or intruders.

Gram continued: "I'm sure there were two of them because, by our pine tree out here, there was one making the same noise. Well, when he shot, it just screamed, and this one by the back door, I could see the shadow of this terrible great big thing. Oh, my goodness, that was the worst thing."

It wasn't until my cousin fired the shotgun the third time that the thing screamed once more and ran off. That time, flame had erupted out of the shotgun barrel, and that seemed to be enough to scare off the creature (or creatures).

"Evidently," Gram recalled, "it (the creature) was there by the air conditioner, probably peeking in at me, because the next morning we found imprints where it had been standing underneath the window. It had smashed the grass down and everything."

My skepticism about local bigfoot-type creatures, which had been eroding for the past two years, was now completely shattered. I had never seen three people so frightened as my grandmother, my cousin and my aunt. The whole thrilling tale really came out of the closet and into the open when my mother, less than a mile away, heard the shots that night and wrote a letter to columnist Barney Fowler that was published in the Albany *Times Union.* His column that day was titled *Mystery 'Creature' of Kinderhook,* and it read in part:

> "No idle talk this: folks in the Town of Kinderhook have been hearing and seeing some strange things. This from a family in the area:
> 'Last Wednesday my mother-in-law, now in her 70s, who lives a quarter of a mile up the road from us, came home about 10:30 PM and around the back of the house came this... horrible scream. She was terrified; it screamed, moaned, made guttural noises, and finally my nephew got his shotgun and fired into the air. It moved away, walking on TWO legs, such as a human would do...
> 'Also, we have seen some large footprints in the snow, and my husband thought perhaps it might be a bear... Do you or anyone have any idea what this thing could be? On talking to other people in the area, they have heard it too.'"

Fowler unwittingly began what would soon become a regular feature in his column – which was usually devoted to news and information for outdoor enthusiasts and sportsmen of all stripes – when he responded to my mother's letter by announcing: "I'd be interested in hearing other comments on the creature."

He created a monster, so to speak. People from all over Columbia County wrote to him to relate their unsettling experiences. A man from New Lebanon, in the northern, more hilly part of the county, claimed that he heard the same type of vocalizations as my mother had described "on a foggy, humid night in the woods."

Fowler also heard from Dr. Gary Levine, a self-styled "paranormal investigator" from nearby Columbia-Greene Community College where he taught social sciences. Levine wrote what Fowler called "a psychic look at the creature." A schoolteacher on Hennett Road, less than a mile from my grandparents' house, claimed to have heard the creature. There were unverified sightings of up to three of the creatures at once near the Kinderhook Creek during the previous year. Meanwhile, tracks were found and the frightening vocalizations continued. Fowler ran these stories through Halloween 1980, at which point, exasperated, he wrote, "Maybe we've gone overboard on this thing."

Nevertheless, whether they were reported to Fowler or not, sightings and vocalizations continued to be seen and heard, continuing in the vicinity of Kinderhook all through the following year, many of which were brought to my attention as the result of some articles I had written on this topic for *Metroland Magazine* in Albany and the *Chatham Courier* in Columbia County. As far as I could tell, no one who reported these things to me were interested in publicity, as many of them preferred to remain anonymous for fear of ridicule. My own father, for example, wrote about his encounter with the creature (or creatures) in his cornfield for Fowler's column without using his name. He hadn't even told me about it, and I was unaware of it until I read the column during that fateful autumn of 1980.

An interesting and odd coincidence was that I traveled to England that October and found that there had been many reports of the so-called "Surrey Puma," a well-known feline cryptid of the area, during that same time. It seemed as though I couldn't escape such reports – not that I wanted to – no matter where I went.

Upon my return home I found that some interesting events had occurred during my absence. In fact, I was beginning to suspect that my leave was required for the creature to make its appearance!

Just prior to my returning home that November, Barry and my other cousin, Russell, had encountered something bizarre on the road near Cushing's Hill. They were walking up the road one dark evening under a crescent moon to meet Barry's girlfriend of the time, who lived in that direction. Just as they neared the corner by her house, they heard something large that was moving through the woods on both sides of the road. Suddenly, *five* shadowy figures converged in the middle of the road. According to my cousins, they were very tall and had little or no necks beneath their conical-shaped heads. When Barry turned to Russell to express his amazement, he found that his terrified younger cousin had already sprinted down the road away from the things. Although he, too, was frightened, Barry soldiered on to meet his girlfriend.

Interestingly enough, Barry's girlfriend correlated this sighting. She was coming to meet him from the other direction when she saw a huge hairy creature walking on two legs that was reaching into the trash can near her house. It was taking out food and apparently devouring it. She had her small dog with her, and the poor little canine was going nuts, running around in circles and urinating all over the road, as if in fear.

In November 1980, my cousin Barry, his girlfriend and my cousin Russell were all taking an evening stroll along with me. We all heard something large moving through the bushes in my parents' field and Barry ran off to start chasing whatever it was that we heard. He chased it out into the field, and we all followed. That was the only night that I think I saw… something.

Mind you, it could have been the reflection of something, or perhaps my imagination was playing tricks on me. Barry, however, had stopped dead in his tracks and was staring at a certain spot in the field. He could see the thing better than the rest of us because he was closer. He seemed transfixed to the spot, "almost in a trance," as he said later.

When I looked to where his eyes were focused in the field, I could see what looked to me like two red eyes. They were roughly six feet off the ground. That was all I saw, and, after a second, they vanished into the darkness. They were there long enough, though, to give me a very eerie feeling, as if we were in the presence of something quite unknown. The creature – if that's what it was, as Barry said he never really saw it but merely felt its presence – disappeared after that, and we all left the area.

After all this impressive activity, I continued my one-man expeditions into the wilds of Cushing's Hill and its swamps; although, I must admit that nearly all my expeditions were during the day. I would have had to have been obsessed to the point of stupidity to trek up Cushing's Hill in the dark if there were as many as five of those creatures lurking about up there. It was an area noted for sinkholes, wild dogs, coyotes and – perhaps now – sasquatches.

In February 1981, I was away again – in Connecticut this time – when strange footprints appeared on my grandparents' property. Gram told me about it over the phone: by the time I reached home, the tracks in the snow had partially melted but were still very visible. I shot a Super 8mm film of them, following them. The oddest thing about the tracks: they ended in the middle of an open field.

The footprints were only about ten inches long – hardly a "big" foot – and they had three toes. They could almost have been the tracks of an enormous duck. They were made by something bipedal. I tried to make casts of them, but the wet snow prevented them from casting properly. While they may have had certain superficial similarities to bird tracks, I don't believe that's what they were. The toes seemed to be sharply pointed and yet very wide, about two inches at the base. It was perhaps significant that we were in the middle of a February thaw when these prints were made.

In early spring of 1981, my cousin Chari was driving along McCagg Road one afternoon when she saw a "reddish-brown… thing" running off into the woods behind my grandparents' house. Once again, it seemed to disappear into the forest near the spring at the bottom of the hill.

Just before Easter Sunday of 1981, Barry's girlfriend was riding her bicycle up Novak Road – the same road on which Barry and Russell had seen the dark figures converging on them – when a "big beast" lumbered across the road and into my father's cornfield. She didn't see it long enough to have a real description of it, as it moved quickly.

On May 8th, 1981, my cousin and several of his friends received a scare in the woods near my parents' home. Barry's friends had set up a campsite down by the creek that runs across my parents' property near Cushing's Hill. Barry arrived at the site later than the others, and he walked alone down the path that leads into the deeper regions of the woods. As it was already dark, he carried a lantern with him. The moment he got onto the path he saw two "glowing" red eyes reflected in the lamplight. He couldn't say how far off the ground they were, but they were high enough to give him a case of the goosebumps.

He went from walking to running down toward the campfire where his friends were gathered. He told them that he'd seen something along the path; they were not surprised in the least. The four teenage boys related that "it" had been hanging around there ever since they had set up the campfire. One boy told him, "Every time we put the fire up, it will get back a little further from the fire, and every time the fire starts to die down, it comes in closer, and it makes these horrible noises." One of the boys compared the sound to the noise a blade of grass makes when you put it in your mouth and blow on it, a squeaky high-pitched noise according to all the boys.

While Barry was speaking to his friends, "it" was apparently still around, so they kept stoking the fire up and tried to keep "it" away. Finally, after a few rather tense hours, they saw the silhouette of something standing on two legs over a ridge. It was tall with long arms and no visible neck. This sighting occurred about 1:00 AM. The thing then wandered off in the general direction of Cushing's Hill. Barry and his band of intrepid campers got no sleep at all that night.

In July of that year, I was doing some research down in the woods on my grandparents' property when suddenly it seemed as though the entire forest was full of dead animals. That's what it smelled like, anyway. A few moments later, the smell was gone. I thought that was weird.

Meanwhile, Dr. Gary Levine, the social sciences professor from Columbia-Greene Community College, came to visit us to continue his "psychic look" at the creature, as Barney Fowler had called it. His conclusion: the creature was hanging around in our neck of the woods because certain members of my family were psychic. He felt that my grandmother and Barry were "calling" the beast unconsciously.

I felt that Levine's tests to determine who had psychic abilities to be rather, shall we say, subjective. He asked Gram and Barry if they had ever had any trouble wearing watches – did their electromagnetic fields cause their watches to malfunction? He also asked them if they ever knew who was going to call them on the phone before it rang. They answered "yes" to both questions. Levine determined then and there that they must be psychic.

It was ultimately Levine's participation in our "monster hunt" that encouraged the crew from the nationally syndicated TV show *PM Magazine* to come and tape a segment for the show about what they officially dubbed "The Kinderhook Creature." During the taping, the host of the show, Alan Taffel, was highly impressed with Gram's sincerity and personality. After he spoke to her, he decided that the segment would not make fun of her experiences, quite the opposite, in fact. He had started out as something of a skeptic, but after hearing Gram's story, his skepticism was eroded, and he took the segment completely seriously.

The film crew visited us over a period of several days. Whatever skepticism Taffel may have had left was further eroded by what happened one night when the camera and audio crew were setting up their equipment for a taping near Cushing's Hill.

This occurred in June of 1981, shortly after I had made a plaster cast of a track I had found in the woods behind my grandparents' house. The footprint had three toes, was 14 inches long and seven inches wide in the middle. It looked very strange indeed, something like the anomalous tracks I had found in the snow. Dr. Levine and the PM crew were quite impressed with this find, so much so that they decided to stay around and shoot a segment that evening in the vicinity of the swamp at the base of Cushing's Hill.

It just so happened to be a full moon, and the atmosphere couldn't have been more conducive to the presence of the newly christened "Kinderhook Creature." As the camera crew set up the equipment, we heard three distinct noises emanating from the swamp just before the camera and audio were turned on. The first sound was something like a monkey's chatter; the second was a high-pitched scream; and the third was more like what has come to be known as the "baby crying" vocalization. Everybody – including friends of mine who had gathered with us on our "monster hunt" that night – looked at each other in stunned silence.

Once the sound equipment had been activated, nothing more was heard – of course. It almost seemed as if the thing knew it was going to be recorded. It was at that moment that we all realized that what had spurred the vocalizations had been the switching on of the big camera lights. It made me hark back to the first time I had heard what I thought to be the creature – when the security lights on the back porch had come on and the response from the woods was that ungodly sound.

In the original version of the segment, Taffel had mentioned the sounds we had heard in his outro to the segment; sadly, that sentence was cut from the final show because the producers complained that the sound had not been taped and therefore the claim couldn't be validated. Just another example, it seems to me, of how elusive these things are.

Our episode of *PM Magazine* hasn't been seen in over 40 years and is now out of copyright, so I present the full transcript of *The Kinderhook Creature* here for the first time:

PM Magazine: The Kinderhook Creature, broadcast June 29, 1981.

Alan Taffel: This is the tiny town of Kinderhook, New York. It is here that Washington Irving wrote his classic, *The Legend of Sleepy Hollow.* Now you might think that any town that has a headless horseman in its history may be used to monsters and legendary creatures. Well, that's not the case. Tonight, we're going to meet some residents of Kinderhook who claim they're being visited and terrorized by a creature that could be described as bigfoot. We'll go on a hunt for this creature and also meet an investigator who is hoping to prove that it exists...

This is the Hallenbeck house here in Kinderhook, New York. The Hallenbecks tell us that over the past three years there have been several instances where they've been visited, virtually terrorized, by a creature they claim to be bigfoot. Now we've all heard about the Abominable Snowman from Tibet, and here on *PM Magazine* we've seen amazing films of Sasquatch in the Pacific Northwest. Is it possible that there's a bigfoot here in New York State? Well, tonight we may just find out...

Sasquatch, yeti, bigfoot: they're sighted all over the world. Large, hairy apelike creature that roam wooded areas. But are they real? You'd have a very tough time trying to convince this woman that bigfoot is merely a figment of the imagination. She's Martha Hallenbeck of Kinderhook, New York and she says that one or more of these creatures have visited her home on more than one occasion.

Martha Hallenbeck: The first time I saw it was when it was down on the lower part of the lawn. I got up really early in the morning, and I saw this big black thing curled up on the lawn. Well, it was really huge, and it was very hairy, had long hair, I could tell that. And, oh, I didn't like the looks of it and then I saw the tracks down there too.

AT: Martha did not say a word about her first encounter to anyone for fear of ridicule. It was when the creature came back a second time that her family became involved.

MH: My daughter brought me home; I had been up at her place, and it was about 11:00 at night. And she and her daughter brought me home. When I got out of the car, I got up on the back porch, and I heard this terrible noise. And I said, "What was that?"

86

And at first, she (my daughter) didn't hear it, and then she got out of the car, and she was frozen to the spot.

Barbara Knights: So, I stood right there, between those two trees, and I never knew… and it was just around the cellar, right around there. The noise was coming from that direction.

MH: It was just so horrible you couldn't describe it to anyone; unless they heard it, they wouldn't believe what it sounded like. It was just terrible.

BK: I brought my son back – my son Barry – with his gun. And I didn't want to leave my mother alone, but I had no choice, because she wanted to stay here.

AT: (to Martha Hallenbeck) What did you do during that time?

MH: Oh, I sat in the living room with a hammer! (laughs) I was watching all of the windows, and I thought, oh, if that thing ever peeks in one of the windows, I'm going to just faint.

Barry Knights: So, I came over with my shotgun, and I had a couple of shells and that, and I thought maybe it was a burglar at first. And I went over there, and I took a number of shots (in the air) and there was nothing. And so pretty soon I heard crackling of leaves and that, and I fired one more time and I heard it scream. It sounded just like a girl. And then we didn't hear anything after that, and my cousin came home.

Bruce Hallenbeck: …Kind of in a state of semi-panic. It was pandemonium going on here, and my cousin had a shotgun with him because he'd brought it over to scare the thing away. Everybody was talking about this thing that had sort of been terrorizing them for the last – I think it had been hanging around for an hour or so. And I was just walking around saying, "I can't believe this is happening."

AT: Sightings like these seem to be common occurrences in the Kinderhook area, but many people refuse to talk about their encounters. Others, like the Hallenbeck family and neighbor Philip Winegard are becoming more willing to relate their experiences.

Philip Winegard: It was just this groaning and screaming, and you could tell by the volume of it that it was a good-sized creature, and then it proceeded to go out to the woods and swamp behind us.

AT: Sightings in the New Jersey/Pennsylvania area prompted this headline…Other countries like China and the Soviet Union are launching their own investigations. There's at least one investigator looking into the Kinderhook bigfoot, Dr. Gary Levine, an associate professor of social sciences and author who was lured to Kinderhook by the Hallenbeck encounters.

Gary Levine: The question of hoax or games, etc. has to be considered. What I have done is that I've examined the grounds quite carefully, and the actual lay of the land - If somebody should approach it wearing a costume or certain types of foot that would leave a large imprint… These particular people are very responsible. There's no kooks, there's nothing out of the ordinary. They are very responsible, down-to-earth people. I think that the observers are very definite in what they saw. They make no mistakes about it. It's an experience they will take with them to their graves. But if one studies the factors very closely, you will see that there is certainly something here that is abnormal. We use the term "anomalistic phenomena." But because we don't know what it is, we should not disregard it. I think it's important, of course, to study it and certainly as time goes by, we inch forward toward an answer.

AT: At one time, science believed bigfoot was the missing link, that evolutionary link between man and ape. However, Dr. Levine tells us that the lack of evidence tends to disprove that theory.

GL: The creatures popular as bigfoot have never been caught. There is no evidence that they ingest food, and there is no evidence that they leave fecal waste. The fact is that they are very elusive. You just can't get near them. You reach them up to a certain point, they elude capture.

AT: Although elusive it may be, bigfoot is leaving enough traces of its existence to keep the hunt interesting. What you are listening to could be the sounds made by bigfoot, recorded in the woods of California. Eerie, yes, but inconclusive as proof of its existence – as are the large three-toed footprints that are commonly found in areas where bigfoot is sighted. Still, no real proof. The Hallenbecks are frustrated by this, if only to satisfy their own curiosities. They spend much of their time now staking out the woods near their home, hoping to spot bigfoot and get good pictures. And we decided to join them, ironically, on the night of a full moon.

GL: There is something out there that is tied in, that has tied itself to this particular family, that has shown itself on several occasions, that by our present standards of classification is not a known animal. It appears to be something that hooks up with these people. There is something here that draws them to it. What is it?

AT: On this night, we do not find out; the only creatures we encounter are mosquitoes. But the hunt for bigfoot will continue, as will the mystery of its existence.

MH: I'd just as soon it would completely disappear, and I'd never hear of it again. That was too much for me. I didn't like that at all.

AT: There does seem to be one common factor to the sightings: Everyone who has seen a bigfoot say they've seen it when they weren't looking for it. When you actually go out looking, you don't see it. So, next time you're out walking in the woods, you might want to carry a tape recorder or a camera or both and get the world's first good picture of bigfoot. We'll be right back.

****

During that hectic summer of 1981, I received reports from all over the county from sincere people who had seen what they thought was the Kinderhook Creature. Many of them were from teenagers or even younger kids, and many of their sightings could easily be disregarded as misidentifications of known animals such as bears – although bears are pretty rare in Columbia County. Even deer can be misidentified if they suddenly appear in your peripheral vision and then take off into the woods.

There was one group of people, however, who really impressed me that summer. This was a family (who wished to remain anonymous) who lived across the river in Greenville, a hamlet in the Catskills. They resided at the end of a dead-end road that was bordered by woods on all sides. The husband was a chemist who worked at a laboratory near Albany, and he and his wife and two children were quite disturbed by their ominous encounters with something strange and unknown.

They contacted me after the *PM Magazine* broadcast, and when I visited them at their home, they related to me that they had had another visitor recently: a black, hairy hominid. They said that "it" only came out at night, and their two dogs reacted quite unfavorably toward whatever it was.

The family had an enormous barrel of fish that they left outside. One morning they found the entire barrel had been picked up and carried down into the woods where it was left by a creek bed. Nearly all the fish had been taken from the barrel. Footprints were found, which they showed me; they were 16 inches long. The chemist had shown the tracks to an official at the New York State Department of Environmental Conservation, who told him, "If those are bear tracks, it's a real monster."

Unfortunately for them, I made the mistake of informing Dr. Levine of the whereabouts of these people, and after his investigations – let's just say they didn't hit it off – they refused to come forward with any other information. Apparently, his tactics, his attitude and his beliefs that the creature or creatures could only be psychically based turned them off. For one thing, Dr. Levine maintained that these beings were never seen to ingest food, as he claimed they were "interdimensional" entities. That is simply not true. There have been many reports of bigfoot-type creatures eating berries and other plants, for example. If this creature wasn't eating the fish from the barrel, then where did they go?

I was in serious "monster hunter" mode that whole summer, and in August 1981, I was awakened at around four AM by a raucous sound emanating from the woods just beyond my bedroom window. When I woke up, I realized I hadn't been dreaming, because the sounds continued after I was fully awake.

The only way to describe the vocalizations I heard during the wee small hours of that morning would be that it was as if two very large monkeys were attempting to converse with one another. Although I had been watching and listening carefully for any anomalies for months now and had heard some fairly strange-sounding night birds and other common nocturnal creatures, this was different. Along with what I heard in July 1980 and in June 1981, this may have been the third time I heard the vocalizations of the so-called Kinderhook Creature.

As I was by this point pretty much obsessed with investigating this mystery, I hastily put on my pants and went outside to look around, but my flashlight didn't reveal anything unusual that morning. After dawn, however, I went back down into the woods and found the outline of something humanoid that had been lying in the tall grass near the edge of the forest, exactly where I felt the vocalizations had originated. It was an almost fetal-shaped imprint. When I laid down in it myself, I discovered that it was about six inches taller than I was, and I'm around six feet tall. Add that to the fact that this is how big the creature was when it was curled up, and you have something that is quite, well, monstrous.

I kept diaries all that year, and on September 8th, 1981, a strange man showed up at the house from out of the blue. The man was a hunter who had been out tracking rabbits near the Kline Kill Creek, about five miles down the road. He had found some tracks in the creek bed that had amazed him. He told me that he had seen my family and me on *PM Magazine,* and he had asked neighbors where I lived. He insisted that I come and see the tracks he had found. I went along, expecting to find some vague markings in the sand, but what I found was far more impressive.

Not only were the tracks fresh and in perfect condition, but there were also several of them leading into the creek. The loamy soil of the creek bed was perfect for footprints and having convinced myself that the hunter and his wife and children – who accompanied him – were not perpetrating a hoax, I made plaster casts of the

The author holding plaster casts he made of "creature" tracks that were found by a hunter in a creek bed near Chatham, NY.

tracks right there on the spot and sent them to the New York State Museum, where they were examined by a paleontologist and a physical anthropologist. They couldn't quite make up their minds about what made the footprints, and they refused to give me an answer in writing. The paleontologist felt they were quite peculiar, and both agreed they were not faked by someone wearing false "feet," that they were humanoid but "odd" and that they were made by something that weighed over 190 pounds. That was a very conservative estimate, I thought, because I weighed 190 pounds at the time and my own feet barely made an imprint into the soil of the creek bed.

All the tracks had five toes, but some of the footprints were larger than others. The largest measured around 14 inches long, while the smallest were only around 10 inches. A mature individual and a juvenile? Seemed likely.

While all this sort of thing was going on, my grandfather insisted there must be some "logical explanation." One night in 1981, however, he had his own encounter with…something. As I've previously noted, he had his tent set up in the woods on the property and there was something outside the tent one night that made him, quite literally, sit up and take notice.

He had been sleeping in the tent when he was awakened by something rifling through the clothes that he had hanging on the line outside. Whatever the thing was, he could see it silhouetted in the moonlight shining through his tent. It was very large, and he was so alarmed that he reached for his gun. He insisted to Gram and me that it walked on two legs. The following morning when he came back to the house, he was still very shaken up. When anyone else asked him what he saw, he would tell them it was a bear. But we've heard that one before, haven't we?

Over the next several months, things began to heat up again, even when the weather itself started to get cooler. In fact, that was one detail I noticed: the creatures were seen more often in late summer and early autumn than at any other time. My cousin Chari, who had been in the car on that fateful night of September 24th, 1980, witnessed something strange in my grandparents' driveway on a night in November of 1981. She described it as "a big two-legged, reddish-brown thing that ran off into the woods," when her car headlights fell upon it. She saw it only for a second, it was dark and so she didn't get a good look at it. If it ran on two legs, however, it most certainly wasn't a deer.

A friend of my grandfather's named Mike Maab, a former employee – as my grandfather was – of the Ichabod Crane School system, was fishing late one sunny afternoon in May 1982 near a dam in Niverville, just outside of Kinderhook. He told me that at one point he felt that something was watching him, and when he looked across the Kinderhook Creek, he saw a creature staring back at him, perhaps 20 yards away. Maab described the creature as around eight feet tall, with long reddish-brown hair on its head and shorter hair of the same color on its body. He said it had small, beady eyes, and, in the bright sunlight, he could even see that its fingernails were black. Man and beast had a staring contest that lasted for about two minutes, Maab said, at which point the creature ambled off into the woods. Understandably, Maab did not choose to pursue the thing, opting to head home instead. Who could blame him?

My next experience with weird vocalizations – I never seemed to be able to see the things that made them – occurred on May 5th, 1982. It was a night to remember for sheer "high strangeness." It happened near the bridge over the Kline Kill Creek where the hunter had found those mysterious footprints.

I was on my way home from work at *Metroland Magazine* in Albany when I decided to take a detour for an informal check of the area. I hadn't stopped at home to pick up my camera or recording equipment; I just decided on a whim to go to the bridge, and, to make a long story short, I was woefully unprepared for what would eventually occur. I should have known better, because the last time I ignored a premonition that there was something strange afoot, I had missed the whole debacle when the creature (or creatures) had invaded my grandparents' property.

In any case, that evening seemed full of atmosphere and mystery. On my way to the bridge, a black cat crossed my path, I saw some bats flying around, frogs were leaping across the road… just about every weird omen you could imagine was present. Late paranormal investigator Charles Fort would have loved the mood. So would Edgar Allan Poe.

Nonetheless, when I got to the bridge, I stopped and parked my car there, just out of the way of any oncoming traffic, not that there was ever very much in that remote spot. I waited for quite a while, not really expecting to see or hear anything, just soaking in the atmosphere. It was my first time there since the early autumn of 1981.

Becoming somewhat bored, I decided to count backward from 100, and if nothing happened by the time I got to zero, I'd go on home. I began my little countdown.

By the time I had reached 50 or 49 or thereabouts, I heard a sound that by now had become somewhat familiar to me. It was the same sound that had awakened me the summer before: like the chattering of monkeys, but with such volume that you could tell it emanated from the throat of very large creatures.

I believe there were at least two of the creatures there that night, and that they were communicating with each other in some manner. It sounded like monkeys or apes attempting to articulate, almost as if they were trying to imitate human speech. These sounds were not made by any human vocal cords, however.

I was so surprised – shocked, even – that at first, I couldn't move. I wanted to get out of the car to investigate, I really did, but my legs wouldn't cooperate. When I finally worked up the courage to exit the car, the noises stopped. I walked across the road to where the source of the sounds had seemed to be, a small clump of trees and brush jutting out from a cornfield, perhaps 30 yards from my car.

At that point I happened to look up, as something in the northern sky had caught my eye. The night sky was perfectly clear, dotted with twinkling stars, and I saw a ball of white light rise into the sky, headed northeast. It was just a small ball of light, something like the size of a peach held at arm's length and as round as a golf ball. It was now going straight up, and it looked as though it had risen from just beyond the trees. It continued to ascend in a perfectly straight line, now far above the horizon.

The light seemed to float, although it moved quickly. It made no sound at all. It moved faster than a hot air balloon but slower than an airplane. Finally, it reached a high point in the night sky and simply vanished, like a balloon popping as it disappeared, but, again, emitting no sound.

In all my searches for the Kinderhook Creature, I've never been so apprehensive or "weirded out" as I was that night. To be alone in the middle of nowhere and to experience something so unknown – and perhaps unknowable – is a very unnerving, goosebump-inducing experience. I wasted no time in getting into my car and heading home.

The next day I returned to the bridge amid the welcome warmth of spring sunshine. This time I took my camera. Sure enough, I found a five-toed footprint on the embankment beneath the bridge. It was small, only 12 inches long or so, but the odd thing was there was only one, and it was headed toward the water. This, to me at least, verified that something very strange had passed near me in the dark of night.

This encounter ended up in a book called *The Evidence for Bigfoot* by two British researchers, Janet and Colin Bord, in the early 1980s. They wrote: "… Bruce G. Hallenbeck has for several years closely followed the activities of the so-called 'Kinderhook Creature,' which has left traces in the form of footprints, headless rabbits and rabbits stuffed into a snowbank as if being stored for the winter. On the night of 5 May 1982, Hallenbeck went out to the woods hoping to see or at least hear the creatures, as he had done before. He sat in his car for a while and then, just when he began to think of leaving, he heard a strange noise no more than 30 yards away."

They then quoted me: "The sound is difficult to describe, but it's unmistakable. For one thing, you know when 'it's' around because everything else becomes silent. The crickets stop chirping, the nightbirds stop calling.

"The sound was a sort of combination of the kind of squeal a pig makes when it's being slaughtered, and that of a monkey or ape trying to speak. An improbable combination, but that's the closest I can come to describing it. It sounded as though there were two trying to communicate with each other.

"Here was my chance at last. My mind wanted to see what it was, but my legs refused to move. It was as though I were paralyzed. When I finally did get up the courage to get out of the car and cross the road to the edge of the field, the noises stopped. But then came the *really* weird part. Immediately after the sounds ceased, a round white light appeared over the field, floated up into the sky and vanished before my eyes. I swear on a stack of Bibles it's true."

The Bords went on to write: "He added that he believed that one of the creature's favorite areas, Cushing's Hill, has an Indian burial mound buried under the thick brush, as he has found ancient stone fences and standing stones in the area already, and commented that the creature could somehow be connected with the mound. This is not a totally fanciful idea, in view of the UFO (earth light?) he saw, and the connection made by Paul Devereux between earth lights and prehistoric sites in Britain. Early man may have marked the major sources of earth energy with stones and mounds, for reasons which are not yet clear to us."

Well, as for that "Indian burial mound" thing, I believe I mentioned in passing that it was *possible* there was something like that under Cushing's Hill, but there wasn't – and isn't – any real evidence for that. Sometimes, when one is quoted in a book or a newspaper, one's quotes take on a life of their own, much to the chagrin of the person being quoted.

The next report I received came about because of my Aunt Shirley, who managed a seed company in nearby Chatham. A reliable but anonymous witness reported to her that two friends of his were hunting in the Berkshire Hills near the town of Austerlitz in the spring of 1982. Despite the fact that it was broad daylight, the two hunters somehow became separated in the woods; not a difficult feat, as the woods near Austerlitz are quite dense.

One of the hunters was amazed to encounter a reddish-brown-haired bigfoot that was, by his estimation, around eight feet tall. He was so frightened that he dropped his rifle and fled. The other hunter finally caught up with him. He attempted to get the man to go back to where he had his encounter to recover his rifle, but he refused. The other hunter was forced to go and get it for him and apparently didn't see anything there out of the ordinary.

The hunter who had seen the creature insisted, "No way it could be a bear." The thing had been standing there not far from him, staring at him, perhaps in wonderment at the huge "stick" he was carrying.

Interestingly, there's a seldom-explored cave in the hamlet of Red Rock, near Austerlitz, that happens to be in an area from where several bigfoot reports have originated. If these creatures do indeed exist – and if they're biological animals and not some sort of paranormal entity – they must have a home base somewhere. In all my journeys up on Cushing's Hill, I have never been able to locate anything like a real "home" for the creature, i.e., a cave or some other sort of shelter. I've found plenty of underbrush, swampland and sinkholes, but nothing like a real hideaway.

My fellow monster hunters and I attempted to perform some experiments to get the creatures to come to us in the early 1980s. It occurred to me that my cousin had made a mistake in firing off his gun to scare the creature(s) away. Previous to that incident, the creatures had been making regular nightly visits to my grandparents' home, apparently in search of food that they took from the trash. Now it seemed that they had been permanently frightened away, frequenting other areas. Our experiments were an attempt to get them to come back.

We modified a birdfeeder in our back yard, taking off its side walls and placing meat and other bits of food on it that were not meant to attract birds. In addition to that, we poured flour around the surrounding grass so that whatever took the food would leave footprints.

We tried different lures, some of which were taken and some of which weren't, but whatever stopped in at the birdfeeder always took the steak that we left out. Obviously, this creature had expensive tastes; it wouldn't take hot dogs or chicken, but it – whatever it was –

always took any kind of steak or beef. Yet it would never leave footprints. Whatever took the meat, it was extremely cautious not to step in the flour, or it had very long arms to reach the steak from a distance. Or it could fly, but it would have had to have been an enormous bird to take the sides of beef we left there.

We once left a couple of slices of pizza in the feeder. In fact, we left the whole box there, even though only two slices were in it. The next morning, we found the box down in the brush at the far end of the property, but the pizza inside hadn't been touched. There were claw marks or fingernail scratches on the box, however.

We pondered what might have taken the pizza box. A dog would have found it difficult, unless it was a very large dog, because the feeder was easily five feet off the ground. Also, a dog would undoubtedly have left its pawprints in the flour.

There seemed to be some evidence that the creature ate small animals such as rabbits. Dismembered bits of rabbits were found in many of the so-called "hot spots" for the creature; oddly, there was no sign of blood whatsoever.

During this period when we were leaving out our little creature treats, I found the head of an opossum not far from the birdfeeder, just the head. There wasn't any blood around the head, and I never did find the body.

Speaking of birdfeeders, my father saw something near his own during the summer of 1982. Around dusk one evening, he saw something standing under the large willow tree in the front yard, near where the birdfeeder was. He described it to me as being "black" and very tall, although he didn't get a good look at it because of the waning light. The next time he looked, it was gone. A thought immediately occurred to me: could the creature have believed that my father would leave food out for him in his feeder, as we did?

Philip Winegard, a neighbor who lived up Mile Hill Road not far from my grandparents, had told me the year before of powerful vocalizations that he had heard emanating from a swampy area shortly after they moved into their new house. In 1982, Winegard further told me that when he had been around 13 years old and living in Greene County, he had been hunting birds in a marshy area when suddenly, as he put it, "a monkey-like creature about the size of a boy rose up out of the swamp and grabbed a bird in its hands." As he was just a kid at the time, Winegard wisely didn't stay around long enough to get a closer look.

Winegard further reported to me that during that summer of 1982, one of his neighbors told him that he had found his picnic table torn completely apart one morning. The man said that he had a feeling of "being watched" the night before when he had been out in his garden.

Also in 1982, during apple season in Kinderhook – a very big deal, because Kinderhook is known nationally for the quality of its apples – a number of sightings of so-called "white sasquatches" were reported. There was even a sighting in one of the Kinderhook orchards. It is perhaps significant that the apples were just ripening at that time of year. The white creature had been seen running through the orchard by a rather surprised farmer. Perhaps the creature liked apples as well as meat?

There were also several reports of a white "bigfoot" that winter near Chatham. I was busy keeping Alan Taffel and the *PM Magazine* crew updated on sightings, and when they got in touch with the Chatham witnesses, they denied ever having made such claims. So much for people being in this for publicity.

There were, however, at least three unverified reports of a white creature in the Chatham area. I investigated the area where the reports had been centered and found that it was a remote spot which was typical of bigfoot reports. It was near a pond in the woods at the end of an old dead-end road. There was only one house on this road, and the teenage girl who lived there insisted that she had seen a white "bigfoot" romping around in the snow in December 1982 on at least three separate occasions. She said she was afraid of the thing, but when the folks from *PM* contacted her, her parents denied all of her claims. It's noteworthy to point out that the girl herself never denied it because she was never given the opportunity to do so.

My parents' first experience with the creature apparently occurred early in 1980 – before the "shotgun" incident at my grandparents' house – but I didn't hear about it until years later. According to my father, he was chopping wood on an early spring evening when he suddenly had the sensation of being watched. He thought perhaps it may have been because his tenant, who lived in a mobile home on my parents' property, had recently told him that something had been "pounding on his trailer" during several nights running. He had called my father over to his home one evening to see if they could find out what it was. On that occasion, nothing was found – except odd tracks in the snow that, at the time, they thought may have been made by a bear.

In any event, my father heard a peculiar noise as he was chopping wood that evening. My mother, who was inside the house, heard it too and described it as similar to the sound "of a pig being slaughtered." Whatever it was, it seemed to have been in the cornfield across the road. The sounds continued, not only the "pig squeal," but "clacking and screeching noises." My father, who had his handgun with him, attempted to pursue the creature in the cornfield, only to hear it seconds later at the other end of the field, which was about eight acres away. Try as he might, he never could seem to get near it.

My parents, brother and sister were all awakened by strange vocalizations at around 11:00 one June evening in 1983. Oddly enough, I was at Lake Champlain in Vermont at the time, aiding Saratoga Springs schoolteacher Joseph Zarzynski in his cryptozoological quest to find the elusive "Lake Champlain Monster," which the locals refer to as "Champ." We had no luck there either.

The vocalizations heard by my parents and siblings had been the disturbing "pig slaughter" sounds, emanating from the woods behind the vegetable garden in back of the house. Needless to say, no one was too eager to go outside and investigate, an understandable reaction.

An anonymous man reported a sighting in September 1983 after he saw "something" stroll out in front of his car as he was driving on Novak Road. He was an elderly gentleman – now deceased – and, at about 9 AM one morning, he saw what may or may not have been a bigfoot amble across the road and into the swamp on the other side. He was so alarmed by his sighting that he drove to a neighbor's house and had the neighbor call me to report it. I tried to get in touch with the man, but when we finally did, he refused to talk about it.

His only description to his neighbor was that the creature was "big and black." When I tried to get a further description, he insisted that it had been a bear. If that were the case, though, why was he so terrified? And why had he asked his neighbor to contact me, knowing that we were investigating bigfoot reports? What really piqued my curiosity was that he had originally told his neighbor that the creature, whatever it was, walked on two legs, which meant it wasn't a bear. The man died six months later, taking with him the secret of whatever it was that he saw.

In October 1983, my father heard strange vocalizations emanating from the nearby woods and subsequently found what appeared to be a "handprint" etched into the wood of his storage shed. The print was discovered a short time after he heard the vocalizations. I took a photo of the scratching and sent the negative to Janet and Colin Bord for their book – sadly, they never returned it, so you'll have to take my word for it that the "handprint" was roughly eight feet off the ground. There were no footprints nearby, but the fact that my father heard the by-now familiar screams beforehand certainly seemed evocative.

Further research by my father and myself revealed a prosaic explanation of the "handprint:" it was made by birds. New markings were found there, and a bird's nest was discovered above the original markings, with a closer examination of the new markings revealing they were most likely made by woodpeckers. So, not *everything* back then was creature-related, although the vocalizations heard by my father have never been explained.

Meanwhile, a gentleman named Walter Brundage showed up at my grandparents' door one day. Hailing from Connecticut, Brundage had read about my family's experiences in *The Globe,* a national tabloid, and was already interested in the bigfoot phenomenon, having traveled up and down the east coast to investigate sightings. A highly educated man, Brundage had some interesting stories to share and had seen some strange things in his home state. A sighting had been reported to him involving a bigfoot crossing the road in front of a car, for example. When Brundage investigated the area of the sighting, he said that he found a huge swath of tall grass that had been matted down by the side of the road, as if something large had rested there. He told me that he could see the imprint of a body in the grass, and that he could even see that the arm had been curled up around the head of the creature. This reminded me of what Gram had told me about the creature that had apparently been sleeping in a semi- fetal position in the yard.

Brundage also related to me that, while traveling through Pennsylvania, the locals informed him that the theory there was that bigfoot-type creatures inhabited abandoned mines in the area. Brundage and I carried on some correspondence after his visit, although I've lost touch with him over the years. I found him to be a very interesting and intelligent "monster hunter."

In February 1984, my father and my Uncle George were hunting near Cushing's Hill when they found some very large tracks in the snow. These were brought to my attention a few days after the discovery, but unfortunately, I didn't have the chance to see them before the snow melted as I had the flu at the time. That's the lot of a monster hunter: he or she almost never gets to see the subject of the hunt.

My father described the footprints to me as "much larger than his own feet," which was evocative enough. Right next to those tracks were the desiccated remains of a rabbit – and no sign of blood.

Speaking of monster hunters, it was around this time that I came into contact with Paul Bartholomew and his brother Robert from

Whitehall, New York, some 96 miles from Kinderhook in the Adirondack Mountains. I don't know how I had missed this, but Whitehall had experienced its own "monster invasion" back in 1976. Now known as the "Abair Road incident," the sightings involved local police, state troopers and private citizens of Whitehall and the surrounding area. The case fascinated the teenaged Bartholomew brothers, who were collecting all the data they could on it. Their research led them to the discovery that sightings and tales of strange hominid creatures went back much further than 1976 in the Adirondacks.

Adirondack Park covers 6.1 million acres, an area larger than the state of Vermont. In fact, it's both the largest park and the largest protected area in the entire United States. It's also the largest National Historic Landmark. Among the unknown cryptids said to reside within the confines of the park are Champ, otherwise known as the Lake Champlain Monster, and there have been numerous reports of bigfoot-type creatures in the vicinity.

Stories of unknown hominid creatures go all the way back to the Native American inhabitants, and the first European to hear of them was none other than Samuel de Champlain himself, who traveled along the St. Lawrence River in what is now upstate New York. During his explorations in the early 1600s, de Champlain heard of creatures that were spoken of so often by the native inhabitants that he felt it must have been some sort of "devil" to them.

At the time, de Champlain wrote in his journal of these tales as told to him: "There is another strange thing worthy of narration, which many savages have assured me was true; that is, that near Chaleur Bay (New Brunswick), towards the south, lies an island where makes his abode a dreadful monster, which the savages call Gougou... This monster... makes horrible noises in that island, and when they speak of him it is with utterly strange terror, and many have assured me they have seen him... This is what I have learned about the Gougou... the tops of the masts of our vessels would not reach his waist."

That may have been a slight exaggeration, but the fact that the Gougou was feared by the local tribes is undeniable. A couple hundred years later, early settlers in New York and Vermont told of encounters with a creature they called "Old Slippery Skin," said to resemble a huge bear but walking on two legs. Newspaper columnist Paul Rayno wrote of this creature in a 1975 edition of the *Glens Fall Post-Star:* "It ripped up fences and gardens, chased cows and sheep, dragged trees through cornfields, threw stones at school children and terrified hunters." The detail of the creature throwing stones is especially interesting, as bigfoot creatures are often reported to engage in such an activity. Raynor also pointed out that eyewitnesses claimed that the creature had legs the size of "spruce logs," but that despite its monstrous size, it was more mischievous than terrifying.

One of the earliest reports of a so-called "wild man" in the Adirondacks appeared in the September 6th, 1818 edition of the *Exeter Watchman.* Under the headline "Another Wonder," the article went on to state that "an animal resembling the Wild Man of the Woods" had been seen near Ellisburgh in Jefferson County, New York. The report came from "a gentleman of unquestionable veracity," according to the piece. The article went on to state that the creature "came within a few rods of this gentleman – that he stood and looked at him and then took his flight in a direction which gave a perfect view of him for some time. He is described as bending forward when running – hairy, and the heel of his foot narrow, spreading at the toes. Hundreds of persons have been in pursuit of him for several days, but nothing further is seen or heard of him."

This certainly sounds familiar to anyone who's read any reports of modern-day bigfoot sightings. A bigfoot-type creature was also reported in the town of Moriah, within Adirondack Park in the late 1800s. There was a report in Schroon Lake, also within the park, in the 1920s, in which a couple named Wright claimed to have seen "a strange bear walking upright."

In 1932, sightings of a "wild man" in the Adirondack town of Blue Mountain Lake received national attention. This wild man, though, was reported to be a human being – although "bigfoot" would have been a good moniker for him, as his footprints were supposedly "nearly a yard across."

The "wild man" had taken the rap for burning down some lumber camps and cabins just north of Lake George. Two trappers, Dick Farrell and Reg Spring, found an old lumber camp in the vicinity of Dunbrook Mountain and quickly discovered that the "wild man" was living in it. After forming a posse with some other locals, they attempted to get him to surrender to them, but he leapt out the window of his shack and ran off into the snow-covered forest, crouching down behind a log pile and shouting, "I just want to be left alone! Go away!"

As the posse got closer to the "wild man," they came to realize that he was, indeed, just a man. In fact, he had a shotgun, and he fired at them. They fired back and killed him. The so-called "wild man" turned out to be a five-foot-six, 160- pound African American who had covered himself against the elements with deerskins and bearskins. To this very day, no one really knows the identity of the man, although he was supposedly carrying Canadian currency. He was buried at North Creek in an unmarked grave in Potters Field.

Reports of bigfoot-type creatures or "wild men" were sparse for many years after that, but in 1959, a farmer from Whitehall reported seeing "a bearlike creature on two legs." In the autumn of 1967, there was a major UFO flap near Ithaca which also involved sightings of large, hairy bipedal creatures seen near a UFO in the woods. One of the creatures allegedly tore a young boy's jacket.

Things started to heat up in the Adirondacks during the 1970s. In the summer of 1975, three teenagers claimed to have seen a five-foot tall creature "swinging its arms" in nearby Watertown. In May of that year, Whitehall resident Clifford Sparks, who owned the Skeene Valley Country Club, reported seeing an eight-foot tall "sloth-like" creature one night near the first green of his golf course.

The Whitehall report led up to the sightings made by Whitehall police. In the autumn of 1975, Whitehall police sergeant Wilfred Gosselin and his brother Russell heard a high-pitched scream that they said lasted for more than a minute while they were hunting near Abair Road. Although they were veteran hunters and knew the area's wildlife well, they had never heard anything like this scream before. That same autumn, two hunters at Saranac Lake reported having seen a bigfoot-type creature squatting by the road. They said that as they began to approach it, the creature walked away.

It wasn't until 1976 that the Adirondack bigfoot made headlines. It seemed to have begun when two boys reported they had seen an eight-foot-tall hairy creature in Watertown that June. Fifteen-inch footprints were later found in the vicinity. That August, another report from Watertown indicated that two teenage boys saw a hulking creature covered with hair lurking in the forest.

The Whitehall encounters, however, really put the creature on the map. Because of the number of people involved and the fact that many of them were in law enforcement, the so-called "Abair Road incident" remains the most spectacular example of bigfoot sightings in the Adirondacks to this day.

Nestled in the foothills of the Adirondack Mountains, Whitehall is a town of around 4,000 people; in 1976, the population was even smaller, but apparently it included at least one bigfoot. That year, on August 24th, Whitehall teenagers Paul Gosselin and Martin Paddock encountered the creature in a field just off Abair Road.

Gosselin later told author and investigator William Brann about the incident when he was interviewed for the book *Monsters of the Northwoods:* "It was about ten PM when Marty Paddock and I saw a large human form standing on the side of the road. We went to the end of the road, turned around and came back. We stopped and heard a sound like a pig squealing or a lady screaming. We drove off to the top of the hill, locked the doors on the truck. I loaded the gun and pointed it out the window. We turned around and drove to the opposite side of the road so I could have a better shot at it."

At the outset, the two young men couldn't make out anything unusual in the darkness. All at once, Gosselin saw the creature standing near a telephone pole roughly 70 feet away. To his terror, the thing began running toward the truck. He recalled that he could barely speak, and he just told Paddock, "Marty, get the hell out of here!"

Paddock squealed the tires, burning rubber as he threw the truck into gear. They made haste for the Whitehall Police, but no one there would believe their story. And who could blame them? The two young men decided to meet with their friend Bart Kinney, who they told about their experience. Kinney decided to go back to "the scene of the crime" with them. As luck would have it, though, Gosselin's father Wilfred, who was a police officer and off duty at the time, also decided to meet with Paul, Martin and Bart and agreed to accompany them to Abair Road.

When they got to the field off Abair Road, the creature was still there.

"It scared me," Gosselin said later. "It scared me a lot. What really attracted me were the eyes on it, big red eyes. It just stood there. It didn't move... It was seven to eight feet tall, about 300 to 400 pounds, and it had thick, short, brown coarse hair. On the head, longer hair. We returned and reported it to the Whitehall Police, who notified Whitehall State Police and the Sheriff's Patrol. There were 11 of us altogether. Eight were police officers."

Wilfred Gosselin and his son Paul strode into the field where the creature had been and heard a terrifying scream. A sheriff shone a spotlight onto the field and saw something walking near the fence. Paddock also spoke to Brann years later about the incident and his description of the creature was identical to Gosselin's: (It) was standing on a knoll not far from the shoulder of the road. I really didn't get a good look at it then, but seeing it later, I would describe it as being seven to eight feet tall, weighing more than 300 pounds. It was muscular, big and stocky."

Kinney, the other teenage member of the group, also confirmed the description in an interview with Brann: "It was about seven to eight feet tall and stooped from the shoulders as it walked. The creature was moving rather slow when I saw it. It was no bear, I know that. A bear doesn't walk like that."

No further action was taken that night, as the creature disappeared into the woods. The Abair incident was not over, however.

The following night, Brian Gosselin – another Whitehall police office and Paul's older brother – had his own encounter with the creature. That night he and one of the state troopers decided to go to Abair Road to see if anything unusual was happening there. Sure enough, as Gosselin was turning around, his headlights picked up a pair of big red eyeballs. He turned off the car lights, and, he said later, "That's when I (saw) the thing look right at me."

Startled to say the least, Gosselin called the trooper on his CB radio. The trooper walked up into the field where Gosselin had seen the creature and turned a spotlight on the hedgerow. Gosselin turned off his engine and waited in the dark. He heard something come crashing through the woods. He turned on his headlights and was startled – again! – to see the creature standing about 30 feet away from him. Fighting his fear, he stepped out of the car and pulled his gun. He was prepared to fire, but decided against it, as he later told Brann: "It was very human-like. You would have had to have been there to understand... All it did was stand there. Hands? I don't know if that's what they were. I couldn't see any fingers. All it did was scream at the top of its lungs. I watched him for a good minute. Then he turned around and started back into the woods."

Despite his fear, Gosselin noticed other details: "It had no tail, and it doesn't walk on all fours, it walks on two, like a man would. It's covered with hair, dark brown, almost black, and on the back end of it, the hair was more or less worn off because you could see the cheeks of the buttocks through the hair that was more or less worn. He was covered with clay on the backside. His arms hung just eight to ten inches below his knees. He walks with a hunch... didn't run, although it could move fast."

Once the creature left the area, so did the two officers. The next morning, Paul and Brian Gosselin returned to Abair Road, and they found large footprints in the field that had a five-foot stride between them. In addition to those tracks, they found another in a stream bed by Poultney River, which was not far away.

That same evening, a Whitehall High School official – who preferred to remain anonymous – reported seeing a large, hairy bipedal creature walk out of a nearby apple orchard. The "apelike" creature crossed the road in front of his car and walked off into the woods.

Yet another report from that day concerned 19-inch tracks discovered near the Poultney River Bridge by a state trooper and a sheriff's deputy. They had the presence of mind to make plaster casts of the footprints, which still exist today.

Sightings continued all that month from Whitehall and surrounding areas. Another state trooper reported on August 30th that he had seen a large apelike creature in the field near Abair Road. That day, an article in the *Post-Star* was published about these incidents under the headline, "Officers Track Creature." The article noted, "Police are investigating reports of a large, unidentified creature seen last week in the town of Whitehall…"

Somehow, yours truly missed hearing about all these reports at the time, even though I was less than 100 miles away. I don't recall them being covered in local newspapers or on television. If I had heard about them, perhaps my surprise at finding a "bigfoot" in my own back yard wouldn't have been so extreme. If only…

The *Post-Star* article included the following information: "It (the creature) reportedly makes a sound that has been described as a loud pig's squeal or a woman's scream, or a combination." That sound certainly became familiar to me a few years later, and to other residents of Kinderhook.

A sort of "bigfoot hysteria" reigned in the Whitehall area for a while. A hunter from the nearby town of Granville reported to the Whitehall police that he had "shot bigfoot." Thanks to Paul Bartholomew, this is the actual police log of the incident:

9-1-76

Reported 3PM off

11PM W. Gosselin

Frank McFarren came and reported that at 11:10 PM he shot four .12-gauge rifle slugs and 6 to 8 .22 rifle bullets at a huge creature that came at him at C. Falls Road. Notified N.S. police

In police shorthand, "C Falls Road" was Carvers Fall Road and N.S. police referred to the New York State Police, who investigated and found only one shotgun shell at the scene. There was apparently no further follow up to this report, as the creature had vanished into the forest. Another story of "the fish that got away."

Another state trooper reported on September seventh that he found 19 ½ inch tracks in the vicinity of Abair Road. That was the last that was heard of the local bigfoot during that particular flap, but there were many more reports years later.

I got together with Paul and Robert Bartholomew during the early 1980s, and we compared bigfoot stories. An article with our bylines appeared in an issue of *Adirondack Life* magazine and our little team of investigators – along with William Brann, another researcher – was born.

We were aided greatly in our search by Dr. Warren L. Cook, a professor of history and anthropology at Castle State College in Vermont. His foreword to our 1992 book *Monsters of the Northwoods* read, in part: "The evidence for the species' existence and ongoing reproduction – if not guaranteed survival – in this area of North America is impressive in its historical depth and for the numerous incidents in the 1970s and 1980s…"

Although nothing quite as spectacular as the Abair Road incident has occurred again in Whitehall, reports of apelike creatures have persisted well into the 21st Century to such an extent that Paul Bartholomew, who still lives there, was instrumental in getting an ordinance passed in 2003 to protect the species. It was a largely symbolic bit of legislation that was passed in part to honor the late Dr. Cook, who had proposed similar legislation in Vermont back in 1987.

Although that measure was not passed, Dr. Cook continued to feel that these creatures – if they existed – should be protected. In an interview with Paul Bartholomew in 1989, Dr. Cook said:

> "My view is that we know so little about the population density of these creatures, that it is possible that the death of one single creature, of any age or either sex, might deprive that particular breeding pool of its ability to sustain itself. The breeding pools are obviously few in number and far apart, so the disappearance of any particular breeding pool, through a wanton act of shooting one, is a crime that is beyond condemnation – it's despicable."

"Bigfoot Bridge" between Kinderhook and Chatham, where creature tracks were found.

After investigating our Kinderhook Creature, Dr. Cook theorized that there may have been a small breeding pool living in the area in and around Cushing's Hill. His theory began to formulate when he heard about my cousins' sighting of three or more creatures together in Kinderhook, unlike the apparently solitary Whitehall bigfoot. He also felt they may have been migratory, as the creatures in Whitehall were most often reported in the summer, but the Kinderhook variety were most often seen during autumn. I'll have more on that theory in the next chapter.

On May 6th, 1984, I found three more sets of footprints along the loamy soil by the place I had dubbed "Bigfoot Bridge," over the Kline Kill Creek. These tracks were quite small, several of them being only around seven inches long and a larger one some ten and a half inches long, the latter of which I cast in plaster. The largest one was 13

¾ inches long and all the footprints were extremely fresh, with five toes. Humanoid but odd-looking.

One evening later that month, my cousin Barry heard more weird vocalizations near the apple orchards in Kinderhook. My impression was that he didn't quite have the courage to go to see what made the sounds – again, quite understandable, as the orchards were shrouded in darkness at the time.

My brother and sister were walking on Novak Road near Cushing's Hill on the evening of May 18th that year when they heard rather disturbing vocalizations emanating from the mist-enshrouded swamp at the base of the hill. My brother remains a skeptic to this day, while my sister is fascinated by cryptozoology and the paranormal because of these youthful experiences.

Gram heard a truly odd vocalization around 1:30 AM on June 1st, 1984. She woke me to tell me that she heard "a laughing cry, like a laughing hyena" coming from somewhere outside her bedroom window. As I dressed to go outside and investigate, I heard the sound myself and it was just as weird as she had described. I switched on my tape recorder, which I kept near my bed, but – do I even need to point this out? – the noises ceased immediately. Before that, however, we had both heard the vocalizations half a dozen times or more. Needless to say, I found nothing when I went outside, even though I walked into the woods, which – when I think about it – was probably fairly foolhardy.

On June 13th, I received a report from my neighbor Philip Winegard that he had heard "heavy breathing" outside of his window the night before. He then heard loud vocalizations that seemed to trail off into a swampy area near his home.

On July ninth, at exactly 3:00 AM, I was awakened by very weird yelping noises from the nearby woods. I reached for my tape recorder and was able to record a dog reacting to the vocalization. I also recorded a whistling sound that may or may not have been part of the vocalization.

The sounds moved quickly and soon faded away. They were quite loud originally, as I'm a sound sleeper and they had jarred me awake. I didn't go out to look around in the dark: I may be curious, but I'm no fool.

The next morning, I looked for tracks in the woods and found none, but I did find the leg of a deer which had apparently been very recently torn off – not cut. It had been placed in the middle of a road being built at the other end of the woods. Quite odd, I thought.

Things were quiet for nearly a year. On May 23rd, 1985, early on a Thursday morning, I heard something banging on an aluminum shed behind my grandparents' house. I didn't hear any vocalizations, but the bag of trash that was on the back porch had been taken out into the yard. The bag was not disturbed much, but my assumption was that whatever was banging on the shed at around 4 AM was the same thing that took the bag.

After dawn broke, I looked around for tracks or traces of – well, of anything unusual – but all I found was a good-sized tree that had been knocked down. The tree was in a straight line down in the woods from where the garbage bag had been placed. It was a young tree that had been almost completely uprooted.

That night, I left chicken and some other foodstuff in the trash, but nothing took it. I put an old truck tire that my grandfather had left lying around over the top of it, and a few days later, that tire had been removed. Again, strange.

On May 26th, my cousin Barry reported a weird occurrence to me. It was so bizarre that I didn't really know what to make of it. Apparently, the night before, he was just getting ready for bed at around two AM when he heard what he thought to be someone playing horseshoes in his back yard, where he had set up the *accoutrements* of that rustic game. At first, he thought it may have been some friends playing a prank on him, because he had heard what he thought was giggling.

He walked outside in his shorts, carrying his shotgun – I'm not a gun guy but Barry is – but at least the gun wasn't loaded. He was just carrying it for show. He looked around and couldn't find anybody, but someone had scored two ringers with his horseshoes.

At the moment he made that discovery, he heard a series of "ay-owt" vocalizations that we generally attributed to the critter. He said there were "three or four" of those sounds emanating from the woods. Shotgun or not, he ended up going back into the house.

He also said he thought he had heard someone or something running on the roof of the house before he heard the noise out back. He thought sure that someone was on the roof. It was possible to gain access to the roof by climbing up a willow tree nearby. He told me, "Somebody certainly must have gone to a lot of trouble if they were playing a prank. The roof is twelve or thirteen feet off the ground. But that "ay-owt" noise was not made by a human."

Again, I have no idea what to make of that story, but there it is.

On June 11th, there were reports of a "wild man" – a *man,* not a creature – on the loose in the Kinderhook woods. The man, sporting long hair and a scraggly beard, had apparently been peeking in windows on occasion and frightening the residents.

Some school children had also reported an encounter with the man, who they said threw rocks at them. Police were called in, but they lost track of the man in the swamps near the Kinderhook Creek. While these reports were not of sasquatch activity, they did serve as an example of how someone – or something – can be observed, tracked and then lost in marshland.

Perhaps the most bizarre "creature" sighting in Kinderhook during this time was reported by Margaret Mayer, a housewife and mother, who was interviewed by author and investigator Robert Bartholomew and me

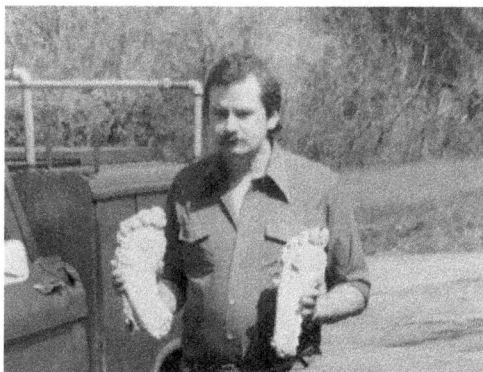

The author holding plaster casts of tracks found under Bigfoot Bridge in 1981.

115

on separate occasions. According to Mayer, she was driving at around 11 PM on Route 203 near the Winding Brook Country Club on the clear, moonless night of Friday, June 14th, 1985, when she saw something unusual on the left side of the road near the golf course. She told me, "The first thing I noticed was the eyes... The eyes were down almost level with the road at first. Then it sort of slid up to the top of the road. It didn't really look like it walked. It was like four or five feet taller than when I first saw it. It stood there for a little while, and it looked across the road, looked in my direction... It blinked while it was looking at me. Then it crossed the road, and by then I was almost to the bottom of the hill. It just seemed to all of a sudden appear on the other side of the road. But the shoulders and the head were like way in front of the legs..."

She said that she mainly saw the creature from the shoulders up and that "it moved fast without any awkward movement for something that big." She continued: "... It seemed to be at least six or seven feet tall when it rose to its full height. It wasn't a person... The eyes were sort of small... but very far apart. It looked straight at me a couple of times. It only moved from the top part of its shoulders and the head. I didn't notice any arms. I could see the top of the legs, but the odd thing is they were very skinny... It looked deformed. That's why I was surprised it could move so fast... I didn't really see it move, but suddenly it was on the other side of the road."

When I asked her if she got the impression that the creature had some sort of intelligence, Mayer replied:

"Oh, definitely... just the way it looked at me, and then it looked across the road." I asked her to describe the creature as well as she could and she responded: "I don't know if it was a mouth or a chin, (but) there was some kind of indentation on the bottom of the face. The eyes were really far apart... almost to the side of the head. The face seemed flat. It didn't seem to have a nose... then it appeared on the other side of the road, and it was gone. It bothered me a lot."

116

Mayer said that she noticed no odor from the creature, nor did it make any sound that she could hear. She said that the eyes were yellow "and the head went right into the shoulders of the body – no neck."

Mayer told me that she had always been interested in tales of the yeti and sasquatch but assumed they were apelike beings. This creature, whatever it was, seemed to her to be more birdlike. Could it have been the creature that left those three-toed tracks in the snow in February 1981? Could those tracks have ended in the middle of an open field because the creature took off and flew?

Drawing made by Margaret Mayer of the "creature" she saw crossing the road in 1985.

During the mid-1980s, reports of the Kinderhook Creature died down, but – and this is important – they didn't die out. On July sixth, 1985, Gram saw two large, round white "eyes" – two sets of them, no less – approximately five and seven feet off the ground near her back porch. After a few moments of hovering there, they simply vanished. "I've never seen anything so bright white," Gram told me.

On July 11th, 1985, my father – an open-minded skeptic - found an odd "stool sample" in his field. He pointed it out to my sister, who in turn told me about it and gave it to me. I don't especially like accepting gifts like fecal waste, but in this case, I made an exception, and I forwarded it to Dr. Warren L. Cook in Vermont. My sister had heard vocalizations in the area where the stool was found, which she felt sounded like "a pig's grunting noises." I don't recall ever hearing back from Dr. Cook concerning the fecal waste, which indicates to me that it was probably from a known animal and nothing unusual.

Fast forward to March sixth, 1986, when I got a call from a Mrs. Johannsen, a woman in her 60s, who lived on Rabbit Lane, about three miles away. Mrs. Johannsen had found tracks near a swamp not far from her Kinderhook home.

I looked at the tracks later that day and found two sets of them between her home and the swamp. The prints looked very odd and were mostly oval-shaped. The tracks in the first set were 17 inches long and eight and a half to nine inches wide. The prints in the second set were 12 inches long and seven inches wide. They appeared to be made by a bipedal creature, and they led from the edge of the road to Mrs. Johannsen's garden shed and around her house.

I don't know to this day what made those tracks. They didn't seem to be tracks of the Kinderhook Creature, as I could discern no toes. And, as I said, they were oval. Just another side mystery added to my investigations of weird happenings in and around Kinderhook.

Here's a real weirdie, not related to the Kinderhook Creature, but an example of the "high strangeness" reported in Columbia County during this period: in November of 1986, four anonymous workers at the Blue Seal Feeds and Needs Company in neighboring Chatham, New York observed mysterious people they said had "no eyes" and that they wore "robes." This occurred in the early evening after the offices were closed and, even though they had "no eyes," one of the robed figures seemed to be staring at one of the witnesses when he (the robed figure) simply vanished into thin air. Other witnesses observed the robed figures near the silos behind the offices. A local deputy sheriff was determined to track down the -what shall we call them? – apparitions but apparently had no luck.

I don't know if this is related, but roughly ten years earlier, I discovered two goat carcasses that had seemingly been thrown off Novak Road into the swampy area near Cushing's Hill. Their horns had been removed – seemingly cut, not torn – and there was no blood to be found anywhere. This strange incident has never been explained as far as I know. Were there Satanic cults lurking around Columbia County? Who knows?

In late July or early August of 1987, my sister Susan heard weird vocalizations in the vicinity of a waterfall on my parents' property. She compared the sound to "crows scratching on a blackboard" or perhaps something made by an "ostrich-like" creature. She also reported that several dogs were barking in that same neck of the woods.

During the summer of 1988, my cousin Barry and I were watching TV at my grandparents' house one evening when we heard a shrieking sound outside. We ran outside and the vocalization was still going on. It's difficult to describe what we heard: sometimes it sounded like a bird, sometimes like a big cat, sometimes like a monkey. It seemed to be emanating from my parents' field across the road, so we headed in that direction, but every time we got near to what we thought was the source of the sound, the creature seemed to be at the other end of the field.

As I discovered later, my parents and my sister were also monitoring the sound, and my mother had the presence of mind to tape it on her cassette recorder. The vocalizations went on for five to ten minutes, but no one could get close enough to whatever was making the sounds to see what the creature looked like.

Ultimately, the vocalizations died down and eventually ceased altogether. But this time we had it on tape. I took the tape from my mother and sent it to Cornell University in upstate New York, where they had something called "The Library of Natural Sounds," which had recordings of vocalizations of virtually every known mammal and bird in North America. They kindly agreed to play the tape against all the recorded vocalizations in their library, and they couldn't match it to anything: not bird, nor mammal nor any other creature.

I had sent the tape to my colleague Paul Bartholomew, who had forwarded it on to Cornell, and I reproduce the response here in full:

Dear Mr. Bartholomew,

In response to your letter of 28 December 1988, I am writing this note. I am sorry to report that after listening to your accompanying cassette, I was not able to positively identify the species which made the sounds. Perhaps they were vocalizations of a captive non-North American of bird or mammal. Most N. American mammals are not very vocal and thus their voices are not well known.

Sorry that I could not be of more help.

Sincerely,

Greg Budney

Curator

Library of Natural Sounds

Since that experience, we (my sister, parents and I) heard numerous weird vocalizations all through that summer, and if I had to describe them in detail, I'd have to say they sounded like a cross between a bird, a cougar and a dog. The noises also scared our neighbors' horses, and when questioned, the owners of the horses said they had heard those vocalizations before.

That summer, I also spoke to an elderly lady nearby who said she knew about such vocalizations but didn't like to talk about them. Sadly, that seemed to be the case with several Kinderhook residents.

My father encountered something in late June and said that he "didn't know what it was." He felt the need to arm himself and investigated. He told me that he saw "two eyes set wide apart, that looked red." He added that he only caught a glimpse of it and felt that it was on four legs, not two. Again, my father was an open-minded skeptic on these matters, so whatever it was he saw – and as an avid hunter who knew all the game in the area – he must have been quite disturbed by it.

My sister took to calling whatever it was she heard "the giant chicken." There was an ostrich that had escaped from its owner on the loose in the region, but it was found shot to death in Altamont – some forty miles away from Kinderhook.

My father was keeping in touch with me about his experiences by now, and he reported to me on July 13th, 1988, that he heard what he called "the critter" briefly on that night. "Giant chicken," "critter" or the Kinderhook Creature, *something* was certainly abroad in Columbia County forests.

On September 19th, at approximately 12:00 to 12:30 AM, my father, mother and sister heard the "critter" for about 20 seconds near their home. They specified that it was making the same types of sounds they had tape recorded the previous June.

"It was pretty darn close," said Susan, "… It sounded kind of doggish last night. It has various series of noises; dog, cat, monkey." There was talk that a neighbor named Mary Brosen may have seen "it," which she described as "a very large housecat" and added that it was "real, real big."

My sister noted, "This would have to be real, real big to make that noise. That's loud."

It should be noted that it was extremely foggy that night, which precluded anyone going out to look for the thing. At this point, our shared opinion was that this may not have been the Kinderhook Creature, but rather something on four legs, perhaps catlike.

A few nights later, on September 25th, my parents heard the "catlike" sound near their home at around 11:30 PM. They said that the vocalizations seemed to emanate from the swampy area down near the creek that ran through their property.

A few months later – on October 9th, to be exact – my sister Susan, who was at that time a language teacher at Ichabod Crane Middle School, was out walking her dog near Cushing's Hill when she heard strange vocalizations which she compared to those in the then-current film *Gorillas in the Mist.* She was very interested in the Kinderhook Creature by this time and was constantly monitoring the nearby swamps and forests for vocalizations, usually with her tape recorder at the ready – although she never succeeded in taping it.

In the merry but scary month of October, leading up to Halloween, my mother related that she heard the "birdlike" noise of the "critter" briefly that evening. A few nights later, my sister was awakened at around 11:30 PM by some sort of sound. Thinking it may have been her imagination, she went back to sleep. About 15 minutes later, her dog started barking and she became fully awake, hearing the "critter" vocalization for what she said was at least a full minute. She noted that it was very similar to what we had recorded back in June. She added that she felt whatever was making the noise was in a field across the road from her home.

On Christmas night of that year, Susan said she heard the by-now familiar vocalizations of the "critter" at approximately 3:00 AM. It was around that date that I found strange catlike footprints and an unusual animal dropping in a nearby field.

Fast forward to 1989, April 14th: Around dusk, my cousin Barry and his girlfriend Brenda were out "scouting" wild turkeys (Barry hunted them when they were in season) near the top of Cushing's Hill. For approximately 15 minutes, they both heard the so-called "Kinderhook critter" vocalizations. Barry said he thought it was emanating from near a pine tree and believed that it was probably some sort of bird, while Brenda felt it might be something else; it didn't sound like a bird to her. Barry had a camera with him but couldn't find the source of the vocalizations, so he took no pictures.

Speaking of turkey hunters, another one (who preferred to remain anonymous) heard the same type of vocalization near my sister Susan's home. He never saw the source of the sound either.

My sister heard the "critter" again on June 20th at around 9:30 in the evening. She was out for a walk not far from her home and said she heard the sound for approximately a minute and a half. She added that they sounded very similar to the sounds she had heard the previous year.

My grandmother also heard strange vocalizations in the wee small hours of the morning on August 14th of that year, and she said it sounded as though the "critter" was right down in the yard. It's interesting to note that my grandfather – the eternal skeptic – apparently heard something in his vegetable garden about a week and a half earlier that he had never heard before. I investigated both incidents but found nothing unusual.

During the autumn of 1989, I received a phone call from one Robert Diaz, a caretaker for an estate not far from my grandparents' house. He reported that he had heard "guttural noises," a sort of grunting, that he couldn't attribute to any known animal in the area. Mr. Diaz also noted that his dog, which would generally chase any animals including deer, would not chase after whatever it was that was making the guttural sounds.

The "critter" was heard by various neighbors on the night of September 28th between 11:30 and midnight. I was able to record those vocalizations, and although one person I played them for suggested it might be a fox, I wasn't so sure.

My sister heard the "critter" once again in the early morning of October 16th at approximately 3:30 AM. She said she was awakened by the sound, which seemed to be coming from the field across the road.

In mid-January of 1990, Mr. Diaz contacted me again to report that he had found several large tracks in the snow which were in a straight line, something he found rather unusual. The tracks were found shortly after a snowstorm and headed straight into underbrush, where they appeared to, as he put it, "end nowhere."

Diaz added that the tracks appeared to have melted and dried somewhat, causing some distortion. Even with this distortion, however, he could make out "toes", and the tracks measured – with the distortion – 23 inches by 13 inches. He did take photos, although they weren't very clear. The tracks went up a hill, and, as he noted, seemed to vanish in the brush.

A week or so later, Diaz contacted me again to report that his son saw large footprints that disappeared into a thicket. They were once again found on the property of the estate where Diaz lived and worked.

During further investigation of the Diaz claims, I found him to be one of the best witnesses I had ever met. A genuinely curious and intelligent individual, he was troubled by some eerie and ominous happenings on the estate. He told me that he had smelled a mysterious "musky" odor on several occasions, which may have been creature-related – as in the Kinderhook Creature, not the (perhaps catlike) "critter" that we had been hearing so much of lately.

Diaz also told me that he felt something was getting into the estate's greenhouse, a 30-foot by 15-foot structure, as the door had been found open several times. He also recalled that it was in the previous May that his dog had barked at, but not chased, an unseen creature.

One day in February, Diaz called me and told me he wanted to show me something that he thought was really strange. He didn't say what it was over the phone, but when I got there, he took me to a spot in the woods in a swampy area behind the estate to show me something truly startling: it was a coyote stuffed into the branches of a tree, about ten feet off the ground. And its neck was broken. He said he'd never seen anything like it, and neither had I.

The cause of death was obviously a broken neck. No other broken bones were observed by us, there were no signs of blood, and the head was intact. There didn't appear to be any skin left, however, and the internal organs had been removed.

It was as if some large creature had placed the coyote there, storing it away for a meal. At least that was the impression we had. It reminded me of the rabbits my father had seen "stored away" for the winter. It gave both of us a very uneasy feeling, and I recall that we looked over our shoulders as we exited the woods.

I never heard from the caretaker after that. I wish he had kept in touch with me, because there was obviously something very creepy going on around that estate. There were other sporadic reports from various witnesses, however.

In late summer or early autumn of 1990, strange vocalizations were heard in a swampy orchard area located behind a housing development on Pin Oak Drive in Kinderhook, just outside of the village. The vocalizations were described as "very screechy." It should be noted that these sounds may have been caused by the four-legged variety of "critter" and not by the Kinderhook Creature.

During the early evening of November 7th, 1990, my mother was walking their dog near their home when she heard strange "birdlike" vocalizations that she couldn't identify. She added that the dog shied away from the sounds.

She alerted my father, and he grabbed a gun – as he was inclined to do – and took after the source of the sounds. He was just as unable to identify the vocalizations as my mother had been. He also noted that the birdlike sounds eventually turned into more of a growling noise.

My father never could catch up to the source of the vocalizations, but he felt that whatever was causing them was close to the ground, not up in the trees as a bird would be. Interestingly enough, a few weeks earlier, I was just waking up very early in the morning when I heard what I thought were the birdlike vocalizations.

On another night in November, I was awakened by something that sounded like – I kid you not – a baboon or a monkey. This was at approximately 4:00 AM and the sound lasted between one and two minutes. I stayed awake from that point on, and about 4:40 AM, I heard the sound again. It shrieked, but mostly it sounded like a big monkey. A very big, angry monkey.

Once the sun came up, I went down to the swampy area where I thought the sounds were coming from, but I found no tracks or other signs of anything unusual. I recalled at that point that I thought I had heard the same type of noise about a week earlier, but it had been so short in duration, I wasn't sure. What I had heard – or thought I heard - on that occasion was a brief growling or grunting sound.

The year 1991 was quiet until March 1st, when I heard another very odd vocalization in the early morning hours. I suspected that our neighbors may have heard something as well, but when I asked them, they said they hadn't.

It wasn't until August 29th that my sister again heard a strange vocalization like that of the "Kinderhook critter" at about 4:00 AM. She said it was very much like the sounds that we had taped and sent to Cornell University: catlike, birdlike, monkeylike. She added that it was very loud, with a great deal of volume, as though it were a large creature. "Quite noisy," she said.

About an hour later that same morning, my grandmother was awakened by what she referred to as an "extremely overpowering" swampy odor that she also described as "sickly." I felt that it was quite odd that my grandmother would be awakened by an odor, but she was obviously disturbed by it.

I should point out here that during this whole period, since August 27th at least, that I had the strange feeling of being watched whenever I was in the woods. My sister had the same feeling. It reminded me of the way I had felt before the Kinderhook Creature outbreak of 1980.

A few weeks later, on September 11th, at about 1:30 AM, I heard a couple of squeals emanating from the woods near my grandparents' home. Gram told me that about an hour earlier she had heard the infamous "big bird noise" that we attributed to the "critter."

At this point in our ongoing investigations, it became increasingly more difficult to distinguish between the bigfoot-type vocalizations and the ones that we attributed to the so-called "critter." Could they all have been made by one and the same creature?

On September 18th, my sister heard a different type of vocalization at around 4:30 AM. This time, she reported "clicking noises" – rather like a tongue snapping – and a series of yelps within 100 yards of her home. The alert reader may recall that my cousin Barry also heard "clacking" sounds made the Kinderhook Creature(s) that he saw in 1979.

I still remember one fine day in October when I was walking on my parents' property down in the woods near the stream when I came across some strange and rather large droppings that could have been made by a bear – maybe. While I was walking near the stream, however, I had the distinct feeling that I was being watched by something or someone across the stream in the woods on that side. At the same time, I saw a flock of birds suddenly take flight and fly away for no apparent reason. I also heard movements from the other side of the stream that seemed to match my own: when I took a step, "it" took a step, when I stopped, "it" stopped. I found this to be both odd and unsettling, and it reminded me again of that fateful day of September 24, 1980, when I had the same experience while walking along Novak Road.

It wasn't until 1993 – in July, to be exact – that I had another unsettling encounter. While walking along McCagg Road one evening, I saw a four-legged creature with strange features crouching on the side of the road. It had long pointed ears, a large tail and was twice the size of a coyote or large dog. It just crouched there for a second and then ran off into the forest.

My sighting of this creature was not unique in the area. Fifteen years previously, a man in nearby Castleton had taken a photograph of this animal or something very much like it. More recently, a woman had reported that she had seen this creature with a bird in its mouth; it had long pointed ears, "spooky eyes," and a long, bushy tail. Furthermore, she said there was a smaller creature of the same type trailing along behind it. She said the first creature was larger than an average dog and that neither of them was a coyote. This sighting had occurred in the Kinderhook area.

Also, that summer, I awoke at around two AM to an overpowering "sewage odor" that seemed to come from the woods. I should point out that there are no sewers in the area. It dissipated after about 15 minutes. As this smell is sometimes associated with "creature" activity, it should be noted but should not be regarded as an actual incident, but rather as just another strange moment during a time that was chock full of strange moments.

In February 1994, I happened upon a line of tracks in the snow that had been partially melted by the sun. I tracked them through my parents' field, and they appeared to be a few days old. Even with the sun-melting effect, the tracks had a six-foot stride between them – a very wide stride indeed. Even more strangely, a line of black stuff that looked like ashes were both within and outside the tracks.

A day or two later, my mother heard the "critter" vocalizations again, during which time my sister – who lives next door – noted that her cats were behaving in a strangely uneasy manner. The following evening, my sister and I walked to the bridge that spanned the Kinderhook Creek – the same bridge over which I used to fancy the Headless Horseman pursued Ichabod Crane – and we briefly heard the "critter" vocalization. To me, it sounded as if there were two of the things.

Another sighting of the "critter" – or something – was reported by a man in Stockport, about ten miles from Kinderhook. Late in the afternoon of December 28th, 1994, a hunter (who preferred to remain anonymous in the report) claimed to me that he was hunting in the woods near the town when he encountered a four-legged creature resembling the one I had seen crouching by the roadside. After doing some research on what I had seen, I found that it most closely resembled – wait for it – a Tasmanian tiger, an Australian marsupial. What the hunter and his friend had seen was quite similar.

The hunting pair claimed they had encountered a group of coyotes or what are called "coy dogs" (from the interbreeding of coyotes and dogs) that appeared to threaten them as they were packing up to leave. One of the hunters shot off a gun to scare the animals away, but just then, they saw a large wolf-like creature – about twice the size of the coy-dogs – with a long white bushy tail and stripes on its body. It ran by them and yelped – and they noticed there was something weird about its eyes. In the afternoon light, the eyes shone red, a pretty strange anomaly.

They felt threatened by this "critter" and said that it seemed as though the coy dogs also seemed afraid of the mystery beast. After one of the hunters let out one shot, the creature yelped at them and didn't back off. After a second shot, the creature ran away into the depths of the woods.

The hunter told me this story because he was genuinely mystified; he had never seen anything like this before. He wanted to know if anyone else in the area had seen it and I assured him that I had and so had at least two other people. I thought the red eyes – which I did not notice in my own sighting - were a fascinating detail, as this was a typical characteristic of paranormal reports -especially red eyes seen in daylight.

An excellent source for Bigfoot reports, the Bigfoot Field Research Organization (bfro.net) features first-hand witness accounts from all over the United States, broken down into regions. Although the organization doesn't seem to include the Kinderhook Creature reports as a category, they do have one account on their website that relates directly to what my family and I experienced.

The encounter occurred in May of 1983 and was submitted by Joyce Gifford. It happened in Kinderhook on Route 203 between 5:30 and 6:00 PM. Gifford was driving with her daughter and making a right-hand turn near the cow pasture on the corner of Route 203 and State Farm Road when the two of them saw a large, nearly seven-foot tall "hairy manlike creature." In the words of the witness: "He was getting up from what appeared to be a crouching position to a standing position. I stopped the car suddenly. It glanced our way and then took off in the opposite direction through the cow pasture. The entire incident took less than five minutes."

Gifford described the creature as having light brown hair, which covered its face except for the eyes and mouth. Her daughter, who was 15 at the time, was quite alarmed, as was Gifford herself. The creature then disappeared into the field and the trees beyond; they got a good look at it because it was a beautiful sunny day.

That was one of the better visual descriptions of the creature;

in recent years, i.e., the 21st Century, I have personally received no new reports of the Kinderhook Creature. Has it left the area to go to parts unknown? Or has it merely gone back into the depths of the forest to escape from encroaching civilizations? I have no answers to those questions, but I live in hope that someday the Kinderhook Creature will return and that someone – probably not me – will get a good photograph of it. And, if not, then at least Kinderhook residents will have an enduring mystery to tell their grandchildren and great-grandchildren. Just as it has been with the Headless Horseman, the Kinderhook Creature will become part of local folklore.

Chapter Six: What's Going On?

In measuring a circle, one begins anywhere. – Charles Fort

Pioneering writer and paranormal researcher Charles Fort was born (and is buried in) my neck of the woods in Albany, New York. Fort was a collector of scientific anomalies – things that shouldn't be but apparently are – and his 1919 work *The Book of the Damned* has influenced every paranormal researcher since. His surname has become an adjective – "Fortean" – to describe events which appear to stretch the boundaries of scientific acceptability. Fort is generally considered to have invented the word "teleportation," among other things, and his catalogue of unexplained events ranging from frogs falling from the sky, spontaneous human combustion and poltergeist outbreaks have inspired countless researchers into the unexplained and endeared him to open-minded readers all over the world.

He was also perhaps the first person to write of alien abductions, opining, "The Earth is a farm. We are someone else's property." He once wrote, "People with a psychological need to believe in marvels are no more prejudiced and gullible than people with a psychological need not to believe in marvels." Fort insisted that he was a collector of data, of "marvels" that remained unexplained by science; he generally offered no theories as to what these marvels were, merely that they *were.*

Fort called his catalogue of marvels "A procession of the damned. By damned, I mean the excluded. We shall have a procession of data that science has excluded." This was a novel approach to the unexplained; most authors before and since Fort have attempted to explain the unexplainable either by rationalizing it – that is to say, giving it all a "logical" explanation – or by coming up with some wild, unprovable theories as to what they are.

I make no such claims; I honestly don't know what these events and creatures are, or what they mean. We can, however, take a closer look at each creature and event individually and attempt to break down some sort of possibilities as to what they *may* be and what they *could* mean.

Let's take ghosts, for example. What, exactly, is a ghost? Most people would say that a ghost is the spirit of a deceased person. But that is by no means the only explanation for a phenomenon that is more complex than one monolithic theory would suggest.

Ghosts can take wispy shapes or can appear to the witness as a living person, as real and solid as anyone. The belief in the existence of an afterlife is nearly universal and dates back to the beginning of recorded history, and probably before. Mainstream science denies the existence of an afterlife and therefore denies the existence of ghosts. But again, nothing is that simple.

In earlier cultures, and on through the great religions that are still practiced today, ghosts – or spirits - are viewed as the entity within us all that animates the human body. Although the human soul was sometimes depicted in ancient cultures as a bird or other type of animal, the general belief remains that a ghost is an exact replica of a living human, right down to the clothes that it appears to wear. The Egyptian *Book of the Dead,* for example, depicts the souls of the departed appearing as they did while still alive, even down to their style of dress.

Although ghosts are rarely reported to be malignant, they are instinctively and universally feared by the living. As the famed fantasy/horror author H. P. Lovecraft wrote, "The oldest and strongest emotion of mankind is fear, and the oldest and strongest kind of fear is fear of the unknown." In some cases, ghosts may be associated with the guilt of a living person, who fears that the specter may be seeking vengeance on them for wrongs that were committed against the departed while they were alive.

Anyplace where ghosts are reported – a house, a graveyard, any old building or eerie location – is known as a haunted place. In some cases, supernatural happenings taking place in one spot may be attributed to a violent or disturbing history that occurred on that spot; not all hauntings take place in areas with a history of murder, suicide or accidental death, however. There are those who believe that spirits – souls of the dead – may, in some cases, not know they are dead and continue to "haunt" the place that they occupied in life. They have not "passed over" into the light and continue to occupy the house or grounds that meant so much to them while they were alive.

Skeptics insist that ghost sightings can be explained away by natural causes, by ordinary physical occurrences. Air pressure, for example, can cause humidity changes in a house which causes boards to creak, doors to swing open by themselves and other anomalies. Peripheral vision can be misleading, accounting for spectral visitations seen out of the corner of the eye. The skeptics also ask why clothes would survive death and why heavy footfalls would be made by spirits who appeared to glide. These are all valid questions and observations. Why, then, do people continue to believe in ghosts?

The great Chinese philosopher Confucius said, "Respect ghosts and gods, but keep away from them." Ghosts are important to many religions; after all, Christians worship "The Holy Ghost," while some Muslims believe that human spirits may turn into demons after death. Buddhists celebrate the yearly "Ghost Festival," appeasing the so-called "hungry ghosts," and Judaism includes the Biblical story of the Witch of Endor summoning the dead prophet, Samuel.

Ghosts can be completely invisible, which is the usual explanation for poltergeists that move real-world objects while remaining unseen themselves. In recent years, ghost hunting programs have multiplied on television, feeding the public's apparently unlimited appetite for excursions into the unknown. Ghost hunters rarely find proof of their quarry's existence, but they have a lot of fun stumbling around in the dark in search of specters.

But what are ghosts, really? Are they indeed spirits of the dead, optical illusions, or perhaps a window into the past? Are they dreams caused by some sort of chemicals ingested into the body – as Charles

Dickens wrote in *A Christmas Carol,* "There's more of gravy than of grave about you," as Ebenezer Scrooge said to the ghost of his late partner, Jacob Marley?

I don't believe we'll ever be able to prove that ghosts exist. If they do exist, it's on some other plane of reality, and therefore unprovable. I do believe, however, that ghosts are not just hallucinations. I know that I have experienced things I cannot explain – the vanishing coleus plant that belonged to my grandmother, for example. The dish of corn that moved across the table by itself. The red light that appeared in my grandmother's room after she had passed away. And those are just a few examples.

Those of us who prefer science over mysticism are intrigued by the virtually limitless possibilities presented by quantum physics. In fact, quantum "ghosts" exist: In quantum theory, a ghost, ghost particle, ghost field or gauge ghost is an unphysical state in gauge theory, a theory that postulates that the physical system being dealt with has more variables. In the quantum world, things that seem solid prove to be elusive; common sense breaks down, and all manner of possibilities present themselves.

Multiverse and parallel universe theories are a branch of quantum physics which could, perhaps, explain the types of ghosts that people see or experience in hauntings. In a parallel universe, what we refer to as ghosts could be people or entities from some other universe infringing upon our own.

In our own physical universe, scientists have only recently discovered that light has a dual nature: it seems to be both a wave and a particle. At times it behaves as a wave would be expected to move, but at other times it appears to be a particle or a photon. And, even more strangely, whether it acts as a wave or a particle seems to depend on us. This is called the "observer effect." When we decide it moves like a wave, it does. When we decide it moves like a particle, it does. We are only just beginning to discover how human consciousness plays a role in what we call reality.

And it gets even weirder: the observer effect moves both forward and backward in time. Apparently, neither time nor space are absolutes as we once believed. Wave patterns seem to be the template for the construction of particles, which leads to the following theory: every one of us is constructed with both waves and particles, which means that our wave selves – the part of us that apparently exists first – leads to our particle selves, meaning that each of us has a dual existence.

The wave pattern, therefore, may be what clairvoyants can see, the "aura" surrounding a human being. Mediums and psychics may be more attuned to a higher bandwidth or frequency than the rest of us. This could be called "higher consciousness" and people who are gifted in this way may be more able than most of us to see "ghosts," which may or may not be spirits of the dead that still exist in some quantum state.

If consciousness helps to create our reality, does consciousness still exist after physical death? Ghosts may seem to defy the laws of physics because they pop in and out of our reality, but that only defies the rules of classical physics; quantum physics includes the so-called Copenhagen Interpretation, which postulates that nothing is real until it's observed. It also includes the holographic theory of the universe.

This sounds more complicated than it is. Let me explain: People who experience hauntings often say that it's as if they're witnessing some sort of time loop, in which the same event occurs repeatedly. Quantum physicists know that for every moment that we experience, a positive wave flows into the future and a negative wave flows into the past in a kind of ripple effect. Perhaps observing a ghost could well be a natural effect of human consciousness.

Quantum physics break the laws of classical physics; while it is the study of the infinitesimally tiny – atoms and protons – these are the building blocks of the universe, and therefore the building blocks of all reality, whether in this dimension or another. Things behave very strangely on those tiny scales. The quantum realm has challenged science; how can something be both there and not there?

Einstein postulated that all energy in the universe is constant, and it can be neither created nor destroyed. If he was right, then what happens to that energy when we die? If it can't be destroyed, then it must be transformed into another type of energy. Could we call that energy a ghost?

Establishment science says that, after we die, our energy goes into the environment, into plants and animals, into heat, into the bacteria that consumes us. But what if there's more to it than that? What if we are, indeed, dual selves, part wave and part particle? Does the wave part live on after death?

Quantum physics proves, among other things, that our knowledge of the universe and of reality itself is very limited. If we have a difficult time proving the most basic premise – the definition of reality itself – how much more could there be that we don't understand? In the quantum world, nearly anything is possible. And ghosts don't seem so very strange after all.

I've often wondered if the little man I saw digging at the edge of the woods was a ghost or some other type of entity. The more I've thought about it over the years, the more I've thought it was something other than a ghost. His build was slight, he was wearing green, and he was digging in the ground for something. All this together suggests – wait for it – that he was some kind of fairy.

Now before you throw this book away in disgust, consider this: belief in fairies is as universal as belief in ghosts. The idea that some kind of "little people" exist in such far-flung places as Ireland, Great Britain, Scandinavia, Japan and of course North America is as ancient as it is common. Why would people around the world have tales of such "wee folk" if there were not some basis in fact?

Now I'm not saying that Tinkerbell is among us. The old legends of fairies, elves and goblins are much darker than that. Most people nowadays think of fairies as tiny humanoid creatures with wings; actually, fairies of the old traditions are sometimes normal-sized people from a higher plane of existence – the Shining Ones – or semi-demonic beings who kidnap human babies and replace them with changelings.

The similarities between ancient tales of fairies and reports of what we now call extraterrestrials are many. Both are known to abduct human beings, bringing them back somewhat changed; when people were "touched" by fairies, they sometimes developed second sight or other psychic powers. To a certain extent, the same happens with modern-day alien abductions; the abductee returns from his or her traumatic experience with a new outlook on life and is perhaps more attuned to that "other" world.

Fairies used to allegedly abduct people for many reasons, but the primary one was to have sexual relations with them. In current alien abduction lore, there is a keen interest in our reproductive systems on the part of aliens. Female abductees have sometimes been shown their "hybrid" human/alien babies after having been abducted, suggesting they have experienced forced sexual relations with the extraterrestrials.

Even the cases of so-called "missing time" have their counterparts in fairy lore; when humans were abducted into the realm of faerie, they didn't experience time as we did. In the fictional case of Rip Van Winkle, 20 years had passed in the "real" world, while only moments seemed to have passed in the realm of faerie.

Who was that mysterious man digging? Was he ghost, fairy or alien – or, in some sense, all three? I don't have an answer to that, but Gram and I did experience something akin to "missing time" when we suddenly found ourselves back at the house, wondering why we left the site of the man digging. And, as I previously related, when we went back to the spot, there was no sign of anyone having dug up the earth there.

All I can say is that it was one of the strangest experiences I've ever had, and it still haunts me to this day. And I wish I could remember the exact spot where he had dug: maybe there's a pot of gold there…

Speaking of aliens, they may not be what people think they are either. Investigator John A. Keel once wrote, "I abandoned the extraterrestrial hypothesis in 1967 when my own field investigations disclosed an astonishing overlap between psychic phenomena and UFOs... The objects and apparitions do not necessarily originate on another planet and may not even exist as permanent constructions of matter. It is more likely that we see what we want to see and interpret such visions according to our contemporary beliefs."

This brings up an interesting point: why did my Protestant cousin see a bell-shaped "blob" gliding down the hill when my Catholic cousin saw the Virgin Mary gliding down the hill? What if whatever it is that infringes on our universe from some other realm shows itself to us only based on our individual preconceptions, what we predispose ourselves to see?

Keel goes on to state, "The UFO manifestations seem to be, by and large, merely minor variations on the age-old demonological phenomenon." Jacques Vallee goes one step further, postulating, "We are dealing with an as yet unrecognized level of consciousness, independent of man but closely linked to the earth... I do not believe anymore that UFOs are simply the spacecraft of extraterrestrial visitors. This notion is too simplistic to explain their appearance, the frequency of their manifestations through recorded history and the structure of the information exchanged with them during contact."

Some paranormal researchers theorize about a sort of "cosmic joker," a trickster of unknown origin who plays bizarre head games with us. Vallee continues: "Human beings are under control of a strange force that bends them in absurd ways, forcing them to play a role in a bizarre game of deception... The symbolic display seen by the abductees is identical to the type of initiation ritual that is embedded in the (occult) traditions of every culture... the UFO beings of today belong to the same class of manifestation as the entities that were described in centuries past."

As for the UFOs themselves, the theories run the gamut: some, such as the Westchester Wing may be experimental aircraft –

although, to my knowledge, even the stealthiest of stealth bombers still makes a loud sonic boom, unlike the silent Westchester Wing. Could some be extraterrestrial craft? It's certainly possible, but it seems unlikely. The objects that Gram and I saw were puzzling, but I didn't get the impression they were metallic, as some "flying saucers" are said to be. They simply seemed to be reddish-orange balls of light, but with a difference: I got the impression they were intelligently controlled. It was almost as though they were putting on a show for us. But to what end?

I'd like to postulate a "what if:" What if many of the UFOs – or, as they are now sometimes referred to, Unidentified Aerial Phenomena (UAPs) are from another dimension? Specifically, what if they are from our own future?

If they emanate from some far distant future, perhaps the "pilots" of these UFOs are our own descendants, evolved into the "greys" that are often seen as their occupants. It would explain why they seem to take such an interest in human beings, both socially and sexually. UFOs have appeared throughout history: you can spot them depicted in religious paintings, historical tapestries, even in stained glass windows. They seem to have appeared especially often when social or technological advances were being made. If they are indeed from our own future, it would make perfect sense that the "aliens" would take a special interest in our species – because they are us!

On the other hand, it's also a possibility that they could be from a parallel universe, which would explain why they appear to jump in and out of our reality, and that they are frequently reported to have not disturbed the air in which they appear to fly. If where they're really flying is in and out of our own universe, they might not be subject to our physical laws, only to their own.

One of the wildest theories – and one posited, if only in passing, by Whitley Streiber himself – is that the occupants of UFOs may be our own dead.

These are wild speculations, of course, and I don't claim to have any knowledge of what these things are. I can only rely on those

139

who have come before me to theorize, such as J. Allen Hynek, who began his career as a skeptic but ended it as such a "believer" that he even had a cameo role in Steven Spielberg's *Close Encounters of the Third Kind* (1977). Hynek wrote, "As a scientist, I must be mindful of the past; all too often it has happened that matters of great value were overlooked because the new phenomenon did not fit the accepted science of the time."

Vallee has an interesting hypothesis which mirrors mine. He wrote, "If they are not an advanced race from the future, are we dealing instead with a parallel universe, another dimension where there are other human races living, and where we may go at our expense, never to return to the present? From that mysterious universe, are higher beings projecting objects that can materialize and dematerialize at will? Are UFO's 'windows' rather than objects?"

These mind-bending theories could, if accurate, explain many so-called paranormal entities, including our old friend, the Kinderhook Blob, a being that certainly seemed able to appear and disappear at will. It's even been speculated that the "whistling" sound it makes – which is not unlike the noise supposedly made by other paranormal entities – may be the sound caused by breaking through from one dimension to another.

There is a long-held belief that paranormal events may be connected to subterranean water and magnetism. The indigenous people of North America were among the many cultures who have long held sacred the magical properties of water. In western culture, hauntings are said to occur at areas where underground veins of water, covered wells and rock strata are found which, theoretically at least, can distort the energy of the earth. These geomagnetic disturbances may, the theory suggests, attract energies – or entities – that may be what we call paranormal.

I've related how my grandfather found an underground spring through dowsing and of how, in a drought year, he located another nearby source of underground water. I have not pointed out how he found an underground spring near his and my grandmother's house as late as 1987 – again, through dowsing. As a result, later that year, a well was drilled and my grandparents had an entirely new water source – and finally had indoor plumbing! Although I may be prejudiced, I think it's the best-tasting water in the world, although those predisposed to kidney stones will probably want to avoid it, as it's chock full of minerals. But I guarantee you that it tastes better and fresher than any bottled water you've ever tried.

And so perhaps it was no coincidence that the "blob" was seen by my friend Jerome next to the old spring in the woods, and that he had to jump over the new water hole that my grandfather had just dug to get away from that white, amorphous shape. In fact, every blob sighting I'm aware of took place in the same vicinity, very close to the old spring and water hole. Was the mysterious blob attracted to that area because of the underground water? If not, then what might be the connection?

Interestingly, the Kinderhook Creature apparently stood outside my grandparents' living room window on the night of September 24th, 1980, right over the spot where my grandfather would find the new well seven years later. Another coincidence?

Now, to the mystery that is the crux of this book: What is the Kinderhook Creature? There are myriad possibilities. The most popular theory as to the identity of bigfoot, yetis and the other hominids that are seen around the world is that they are a species of large bipedal apelike beings that are so far undiscovered by science. They may be related to the prehistoric ape Gigantopithecus, the bones of which have been found in Asia. This may not be as unlikely as it seems: the mountain gorilla, for example, was not discovered until the late 19th Century. Of course, they live in equatorial Africa, a far cry from the Pacific Northwest, or, for that matter, upstate New York.

Another theory postulates that they could be psychic projections akin to poltergeists and hauntings. I've never found that theory especially compelling; people are obviously seeing something real. They could, in some cases, be seeing something they have simply misidentified, such as a bear. A person brought up in a city may not be used to seeing animals such as a bear, a moose or even a deer. On the other hand, most bigfoot sightings around the country are made by people who live in rural areas and are accustomed to such wild animals. Some reports are even made by experienced hunters who aren't likely to mistake a bear for a bigfoot.

Apes have occasionally escaped from zoos, but, as bigfoot reports come from all around the country (and the world), they would have to be escaping on a mass scale, so we can pretty much rule that out, generally speaking. There may occasionally be a report of an escaped chimpanzee on the loose (which might have been the basis for reports of an "ape" on Long Island in 1931), but I'm guessing they're rare.

Pranksters dressed in bigfoot costumes? That has happened on occasion. There have certainly been hoaxes, especially some alleged bigfoot videos. Again, however, these are few and far between; besides, how many people would be willing to put on a costume, run out into the woods and risk being shot by an alarmed hunter?

As to why these creatures remain so elusive, here's a hypothesis: what if these creatures had a highly evolved set of defense mechanisms that allowed them to adapt to their surroundings in the same way that a chameleon changes color to blend into its environment?

Then there are the more exotic explanations: could they be interdimensional beings that come from another plane of existence, another dimension from which they can appear in our reality and then disappear at will? Pretty far-fetched, I admit, but that would explain the mysterious set of footprints that suddenly stopped dead in the middle of a field.

Bigfoot as extraterrestrials? Again, exotic and with very little circumstantial evidence, although the creatures have occasionally been sighted in the vicinity of UFOs. The creatures have also been claimed to be demonic manifestations, mainly because they're sometimes reported to have red eyes – a demonic trait. Again, virtually no evidence otherwise.

Mass media sensationalism may have something to do with it. Bigfoot reports (and for that matter, reports of UFOs, the Loch Ness Monster and a host of other anomalies) tend to go in "waves," or as investigators call them, "flaps." A certain amount of mass hysteria may be involved: one or two people see something they can't explain, it gets printed or broadcast in the media and then everybody and his brother claim to see the same thing. It may be wish fulfillment: it's fun and exciting to see a bigfoot, especially in this drab and often grim world of politics, wars and tragedy.

I can pretty much guarantee that the vast majority of bigfoot reports are not hallucinations reported by mentally unbalanced people. The skeptics who believe that have obviously never really studied the subject or they would know that most bigfoot reports come from solid citizens who have nothing to gain – and often plenty to lose – by making such reports public. The ridicule they often endure far outweighs any benefits they may receive.

Media sensationalism may feed mass hysteria. Research on the topic indicates that when a group of people with common beliefs encounters something ambiguous in a "mysterious" environment such as a dark wooded area and they hear an unexpected noise – which could be anything from a vocalization to the rustling of brush – the common impulse is the desire to know what made the sound. If it's a friend walking nearby, they can relax. If it's bigfoot, on the other hand, they can hightail it out of there.

No one likes to make a fool of him or herself if they run away screaming from what turns out to be their six-year-old brother in the brush. It's possible, however, that people camping out in the wilderness may be in the bigfoot "mind set." Under those conditions, they would be suggestible and, perhaps, prone to misinterpretations. If people are camping in an area where bigfoot has been reported and they hear a raccoon climbing a tree and making a noise, some of the group may see two eyes in the darkness looking down at them from seven or eight feet off the ground; a raccoon's eyes may appear large and pinkish-red when a flashlight is shone on them. Almost immediately, the group imagination fills in the blanks and deduces it's a bigfoot staring at them. As the witnesses scream and run, their compatriots – who may also be in a "bigfoot" frame of mind – do the same.

It seems likely that some bigfoot sightings are the result of mass hysteria, but certainly not all. Far too many cases involve multiple witnesses who saw the creature clearly at close range – within 30 yards, for example – for that to be the case. There have also been many cases, such as those in Whitehall, in which the sightings have been made by trained police officers. Nevertheless, eyewitness testimony has often been proven to be inaccurate. This is why most scientists refuse to accept the existence of bigfoot or, at the very least, are extremely skeptical. Since the body – or indeed any indisputable physical evidence – of a bigfoot has yet to be produced, skepticism by mainstream science is understandable. All which we researchers have so far are eyewitness reports, footprints and some rather fuzzy films and videos (although I've always found the famous Patterson/Gimlin film to be very convincing).

A fossil or a body can't be faked without being proven a hoax; it's that simple. And again, mass hysteria can't explain all the sightings, no matter how skeptical one wants to be; huge naked footprints have been found in the vicinity of bigfoot reports, some of them tracking for miles in the wilderness. They often appear to have been made by something much heavier than a human being. It's hard to believe there would be so many pranksters about who would go to such extremes just to play a prank. And if there are so many pranksters out there, where are they and why have so few of them been revealed?

One of the most interesting things about bigfoot sightings is that the creatures don't really conform to expectations of what such a huge, threatening-looking creature should do. Instead of terrorizing or threatening the witnesses, they are often described as behaving timidly, quite unconcerned about the witness. Whether they're crossing a road or simply walking in the woods, these creatures certainly don't behave in the way they're portrayed in the movies.

144

There's a 2006 horror movie called *Abominable,* for example, in which a bigfoot literally tears a person in half. Nothing even close to that sort of behavior has ever been described by an eyewitness.

Researcher Robert E. Bartholomew provided some insight in the 1992 book *Monsters of the Northwoods,* co-authored by himself, his brother Paul Bartholomew, Bill Brann and yours truly as to why few scientists – aside from Jane Goodall and one or two others – consider bigfoot to be "real." Robert Bartholomew wrote: "Seemingly honest, intelligent, mentally healthy people worldwide report encounters with supernatural creatures daily. Malaysians meet Toyl spirits who are typically just a few inches tall. The Ojibway Indians of Ontario, Canada continue to see thunderbirds the size of airplanes, while modern day encounters with bunyips have been reported by Australian aborigines. The numerous animist cultures who believe in various in-dwelling nature spirits frequently report encountering such entities. In many western cultures, bigfoot-like creatures are sighted annually. What does it all mean? Is there some deep-seated psychological need to believe in 'monsters' – so much so that our imaginations create them? Could these beings exist as some unknown life form evolving remarkable abilities which allow it to elude capture? Could these sightings be of creatures from another dimension or planet? There is fascinating circumstantial evidence that these creatures exist.

> *At the least, this study provides insight into the making of a modern myth and helps to dispel the erroneous belief that many witnesses or believers in 'monsters' are mentally unbalanced. At best, if true, it documents one of the most startling and important events in human history. While I hope that bigfoot and other phantom creatures exist, and find much of the evidence intriguing, I cannot accept their reality until concrete proof is uncovered that will convince the scientific community; nothing short of a body, bones or fossilized remains. Eyewitness testimony, footprints, ambiguous hair*

strands and photographs are interesting, but unconvincing,
unacceptable scientific evidence. People once reported fairy
and witch sightings by the thousands. There were even
'abductees' to fairyland and witch sabbaths. Similar parallels
can be made with the widespread belief in spiritualism during
the latter 19th Century. While the notion that fairies or witches
exist today seems laughable, the point is – seemingly honest,
reliable people raised in an environment that promises the
reality of fairies and witches saw what they expected to see.
Even hallucinations reflected the prevailing belief. This does
not mean that bigfoot does not exist. But it does help to explain
why the scientific community has yet to accept bigfoot's
existence. Remarkable claims require clear, non-
circumstantial evidence. Time, and adherence to the scientific
method will ultimately determine whether bigfoot exists or if it
belongs to the realm of folklore and social psychology, as a
monster of the human mind.

What about the defense mechanism, which postulates that the creatures can blend in with their immediate surroundings? There are certain types of lizards, fish and frogs – not to mention many insects – that can change color to blend in with the flora that surrounds them; this is an evolutionary development that's a means of protecting them from predators. Bigfoot creatures may have evolved – and I stress the word "may" – to have similar but yet understood defense mechanisms. This would explain why so many people claim they've seen a bigfoot, yet searches of the area uncover nothing.

This possibility leads to some interesting speculation. What happens to such creatures when they die? Presumably, they aren't immortal, so where do their remains go? Some researchers theorize that bigfoot-type creatures may bury their dead, as even the earliest humans were known to have done. This may seem far-fetched to some, but there are ancient traditions in some Native American tribes that the creatures do just that. Other lines of thought include possible post-mortem cannibalism: in other words, that the creatures eat their own dead. It's a gruesome but not unreasonable explanation as to why no bones have ever been found.

The late Dr. Gary Levine, who investigated the Kinderhook Creature, posited, "It seems to be a paranormal phenomenon which is related to psychic powers… Some people who are psychic can draw this creature to them."

Levine, who personally investigated other bigfoot and UFO cases, had no patience with the theory that bigfoot creatures were "ape men" or related in some way to Gigantopithecus. In fact, he didn't believe they were even biological creatures as we know them. He claimed that what we were dealing with "has no basis in evolution. It's not an animal that's been somehow hiding in the mountains for thousands of years and then suddenly comes down. But it is here, and it's drawn to us in a psychic fashion. It appears to be a creation, a projection, of our collective imaginations. It has a form, but our perception of it is exactly what we think it should look like."

Investigators and authors Loren Coleman and Jerome Clark theorized that our thoughts can sometimes take on physical form in their book *Creatures of the Outer Edge.* They wrote: "If the otherworld is really the domain of the collective unconscious imprinted on the 'psi field,' creating in each cultural frame of reference a dream world… fixed in the psychic realm, then… Where peasants were kidnaped into fairyland and mystics were transported into Heaven, today UFO contactees are whisked off to Venus, a world as full of scientific marvels as the others were of supernatural ones."

I've already noted how my Protestant cousin and my Catholic cousin saw two different forms of the "blob," but how does this apply to bigfoot sightings? For one thing, it could explain the footprints that stop dead in the middle of a field and the lack of physical proof of the creatures' existence. Could such things be interdimensional entities – or interplanetary?

I recounted in Chapter Five of how I heard weird vocalizations near "Bigfoot Bridge" and of how, seconds later, a white light flew up from the horizon and vanished into the sky. Now we are venturing into bigfoot sightings of high strangeness, of which my own experience was only one small example. There was a similar account from Roachdale, Indiana in August of 1972, when a woman and her infant son heard a "deep howl." Roughly an hour and a half earlier, a luminous object had appeared over their neighbor's cornfield, briefly hovered there and then "just sort of blew up," leaving no trace at all. That's exactly what seemed to happen to the white light I saw.

But the Indiana event got much weirder: during the next few nights the woman, her husband and her son heard strange "pounding" sounds and saw a "broad-shouldered, six-foot-tall, black and hairy bipedal creature" that ran into the cornfield. It smelled like "dead animals or garbage" and stood like a man but would sometimes run on all fours – without leaving any tracks. Sometimes, the witnesses said, "It looked like you could see through it."

Observations of bigfoot activity related to UFOs is uncommon, but far from unheard of. In October 1973, again in Indiana, a fisherman observed an apelike creature from a distance that was also watching *him,* similarly to the way the Kinderhook Creature allegedly observed fisherman Mike Maab. After losing the creature from his sight, he later said that it startled him when it suddenly touched his shoulder. He reported that he had whirled around when the thing had touched him and that it ran away incredibly fast, leaping over a deep ditch and vanishing into the woods. Shortly after, he observed a "glowing bronze object" that shot into the sky and quickly faded from sight. The following evening, the fisherman and four of his friends drove to the area – and they were trailed all the way there by "a white, glowing starlike light" that vanished near a bridge close to the original sighting spot. Then, to their shock, they all saw an eight -to -nine-foot-tall creature standing in some high weeds, motionless "as if in a trance." The witnesses hollered to the creature and threw rocks at it, but it stood stock still. They noted that it gave off a musty odor and that, strangely, its presence didn't seem to faze the crickets, frogs and other nocturnal animals at all. They also noticed that their flashlight beams seemed "weaker" when they flashed onto the creature, which finally disappeared while they moved their vehicles off the road.

These reports suggest that what the witnesses were seeing was either of extraterrestrial, interdimensional or psychic origin. Mind you, none of those theories is close to being proven. The very existence of psychic projection, for example, is still the subject of intense scientific debate. This is because these abilities have not been shown to be replicated under strict laboratory conditions, which leads many researchers to believe that so-called "psychics" may in fact be hoaxers.

In recent years, there have been growing investigations into the field of so-called "altered states." The short version implies that most bigfoot sightings are vague and, perhaps, misperceptions or ordinary phenomena. In the relatively few vivid, close-up encounters, most have supposedly happened to people in rural or wilderness areas at night, the very conditions that are conducive to visions and hallucinations. These conditions combined with fatigue, emotional or physical stress, fasting, drug use, meditation or sleep deprivation can cause dreamlike experiences.

On the other hand, if bigfoot reports represent dreamlike visions, why do the descriptions of the creatures all have such similarities? One would expect individual reports to include more than the seven- to eight-foot-tall hairy, bipedal apelike creatures. And if the sightings are influenced by cultural beliefs ala the Kinderhook blob, why aren't bigfoot sightings around the world more varied? There are differences that suggest slightly different types, with the Himalayan yeti having long shaggy hair and the Chinese wild man somewhat shorter than the "average" bigfoot. But aside from those minor differences, reports from around the world – from the Australian yowie to the Russian alma – describe remarkably similar creatures that seem to behave in almost identical ways. Shy, retiring and ignoring human beings as much as possible, they reportedly behave in ways that real biological animals would.

From ancient times on up to today, the belief has held that fasting and sleep deprivation may fatigue the body and mind while in isolated environments, creating so-called "magical" experiences. These situations are not involved in all bigfoot reports, however. As we have seen, there are a great many cases in which multiple witnesses were involved. Characteristics of altered states may involve bright lights and time either seeming to slow down or speed up, but none of the bigfoot cases that are covered in this book involve these elements. And, although this shouldn't need to be pointed out, hallucinations and altered states do not produce footprints.

Anthropologist Warren Cook, who investigated the Kinderhook Creature in the 1980s and 1990s and who felt there may be a small breeding pool of bigfoot creatures in the vicinity of Cushing's Hill.

The late Dr. Warren Cook, who investigated the Kinderhook Creature as well as reports from Whitehall and Vermont, felt that the evidence for bigfoot pointed toward flesh and blood biological creatures. Cook was one of the few serious academic researchers involved in this subject during the 1980s, and his working theory was that the creatures that were being observed in the northeastern corner of the United States may have been relic survivors of *Australopithecus,* apelike beings that walked the earth about half a million years ago.

In the June sixth, 1984, edition of the Rutland (Vermont) *Daily Herald,* an article under the headline of "Cook Keeps Eye on Recent Bigfoot Sighting," Dr. Cook was quoted extensively. The article by Tom Mitchell began:

> *Recent reports of activity that is believed to be caused by a legendary ape-like creature in the towns of Whitehall, NY and Kinderhook, NY have sparked the interest of local anthropologist Dr. Warren Cook.*

During the past year, Cook, a member of the Castleton State College Faculty, has researched reports from California of a large creature known as Sasquatch.

The large creatures, who some believe are a relative of man, have also been called bigfoot, yeti, swamp ape and bushman...

The article went on to chronicle my family's and my experiences with the Kinderhook Creature and continued: "Cook has kept informed concerning reports of bigfoot activity in New York. Saying reports of bigfoot encounters should not be laughed at, Cook said he wanted to know of any similar future sightings. From the article:

Cook refers to places where the creature is reported to be abundant as 'hot spots.' Cook said he believed the creature could exist in Vermont.

The bigfoot creature's supposedly strong sense of smell and knowledge of its territory make it particularly elusive, said Cook. The creature is also a nocturnal one, added Cook.

Some researchers say efforts should be made to shoot one of the creatures to enable the body to be studied by scientists. However, Cook disagrees.

Cook said he did not think the creatures would harm humans and needed to be protected from extinction.

"Killing one for the sake of establishing the species' existence might tip the scales against survival of a limited breeding pool," said Cook...

Cook said he believed the sasquatch creature appeared to be the closest living relative to mankind.

He said the bigfoot creature was similar to a variety of Australopithecus, a genus of extinct primates, represented by a skull found in South Africa.

There were a few other anthropologists who agreed with Cook in those days, notably Dr. Grover Krantz of Washington State University, a world-renowned cryptozoologist who once took a quick look at the plaster casts I had made of the Kinderhook Creature when I attended a cryptozoological conference in New York City. When I showed them to him, the *paparazzi* started snapping photos; I wish I knew what had happened to all those photos! After looking at the casts for a few moments, Krantz admitted they were "very interesting," but told me – somewhat to my disappointment – that he already had enough to worry about with reports in his home state of Washington without taking on such encounters on the east coast. And, with that, he had to move on.

Krantz held a controversial opinion that the only way science would be able to prove the existence of these creatures would be to obtain a body by killing one. This was an idea that horrified many researchers – including Dr. Cook – who felt that the creatures we know as bigfoot should be left alone.

Throughout history, there are numerous examples of species that were previously unknown to science that have been discovered completely unexpectedly. Author John A. Keel wrote of the first Caucasian to see a gorilla in Africa: "Scientists had a laugh in 1856, when Paul du Chaillu returned from the Congo and described his encounter with a hairy giant. 'He stood about a dozen yards from us and was a sight I think I shall never forget,' du Chaillu reported. 'Nearly six feet high, with immense body, huge chest and great muscular arms, with fiercely glaring large deep gray eyes… he stood there and beat his breast with his huge fist till it resounded like an immense bass drum."

The most famous case of a species thought to be extinct – but wasn't – regarded the discovery of a coelacanth, a fish believed to have been extinct for 60 to 70 million years, which was brought up alive in a fisherman's net off the coast of South Africa on December 22, 1938. The gorilla and the coelacanth, of course, were discovered on or near the African continent, where many remote areas still exist. Why has bigfoot, which allegedly exists in more civilized regions, so far eluded capture or even verification of its existence?

In *Creatures of the Outer Edge,* Clark and Coleman ask this question: "…Why, if they are real, are there no bodies, no bones, no live specimens locked securely in zoos and laboratories? Why only certain kinds of physical evidence, invariably of a somewhat ambiguous nature – footprints, strands of hair or fur, possible feces samples, and not others? The 'evidence' we have is always just enough to keep us from rejecting the reports as delusions but never enough to prove conclusively that unknown animals exist in our midst."

This is extremely frustrating for researchers, but the fact is, whatever these unknown creatures are, they may represent a phenomenon that is beyond our ability to understand. If bigfoot is biological rather than paranormal, then researchers should be concerned about its preservation. If such creatures do exist in what we call reality and are flesh and blood like us, it's unfortunate that mainstream science will not accept their existence without having a body to dissect.

If, on the other hand, these creatures exist only on the "outer edge" of reality as Clark and Coleman postulate, then we have a whole different level of research to conduct. Bigfoot reports include a small number of reports in which the creature sighted doesn't behave like a flesh and blood animal. In autumn 1968 there was a bizarre sighting in Point Isabel, Ohio in which three witnesses claimed to have seen what they called a "monster" rise from the underbrush and walk toward them. As this was a nighttime sighting – at around 10 PM – it must have been truly frightening, as they described the creature as around ten feet tall and with extremely broad shoulders roughly four feet wide. They claimed the creature was hairy, with apelike arms and glowing eyes, protruding teeth and pointed ears. When one of the witnesses took a shot at it, the thing let out a scream and was suddenly enveloped in a white mist. After a few seconds, the creature had vanished and so had the mist.

Another case in Uniontown, Pennsylvania in 1974 involved a seven-foot-tall apelike creature that, when shot at, "disappeared in a flash of light…just like someone taking a picture." Later, a group of four or five of the creatures with "fire red eyes that glowed" were spotted.

Let's say for the sake of argument that at least some of these sightings involve interdimensional entities: if that's the case, why are they visiting this dimension at all – and why are they running around in the woods? If they have an ability to appear and disappear at will, why is it that in most cases they're seen running or walking away? Why don't they all just vanish into that other dimension if they feel threatened? All of which begs the question: just what is another dimension, and does it in fact exist?

So many questions and so few answers. Perhaps there are both biological primates that remain undiscovered – and there are also paranormal beings that we just don't understand, which are seen only when two dimensions intersect. Some bigfoot reports certainly have paranormal undertones, but most do not. Most sightings are quite mundane, with the creatures crossing roads or just walking in the woods, minding their own business.

I don't pretend to know what these things are. As is the case with most monster hunters, I've never actually seen my quarry. But I do know that something strange is out there. I've had experiences that I would classify as paranormal, i.e., unexplained and unexplainable, and I've had experiences that I would call cryptozoological. Looking back on those heady days of the early 1980s, when the Kinderhook Creature was seen by dozens of individual witnesses, it seems impossible that it all happened. Yet it did. Finding bigfoot literally in one's own backyard changes one's perception of reality. It opens the mind and, in some respects, delights the senses, bringing back a sense of childhood wonder. In a way, when the creature was at large, it felt as though Santa Claus was real after all.

I'll leave my beloved grandmother the last word. At first, as she told *PM Magazine*, she said she hoped she would never experience such a thing again. Toward the end of her life, though, she changed her tune and said to me more than once, "I wish bigfoot would come back. Those were exciting times, weren't they?"

Epilogue

On the afternoon of Monday, August 22nd, 2022 – a few days before I completed the writing of this book – my mother, now 86 years young and still sharp as a tack, saw an animal she didn't recognize out her kitchen window. It was a four-legged creature, light brown in color, that was meandering between the nearby woods and the house. As it turned in her direction, she saw what it was: a catamount, otherwise known as a mountain lion, roughly the size of a large dog. It then wandered off in the direction of my sister's house next door, and then up the hill into the woods.

According to the New York State Department of Environmental Conservation, catamounts are not supposed to exist in New York. This proclamation doesn't prevent people from seeing them, however, and one of my mother's neighbors – the son of the man who saw "something" cross the road in front of his car in the early 1980s that he claimed at that time walked on two legs – has also seen the catamount.

This same gentleman also told my parents that "something" – he thinks it was a bear, although he hasn't seen it – got up onto his front porch recently and made a mess of things, tearing up items that he had on the porch and generally causing havoc. He believes it to be a bear, and maybe it is. Maybe.

Nearly every night, Rosa and I hear something banging on the aluminum shed next to the house. As the shed contains the furnace and nothing else, it's difficult to say why an animal would want to get in there, especially on warm summer nights. I've looked around for any tracks or other evidence of some sort of animal near the shed but have so far found nothing.

The key to unlocking these mysteries is pure human curiosity. Homo Sapiens has always had a fascination with the unknown. We're drawn to it in spite of the fact that we sometimes fear it. Someday, perhaps, at least a few of these mysteries will be solved. Meanwhile, they tantalize, tease and occupy our minds.

I strongly suspect that the paranormal and the cryptozoological will follow me to the end of my life.

And perhaps beyond.

Bibliography

Books

Bartholomew, Paul and Robert, Brann, William, Hallenbeck, Bruce: *Monsters of the Northwoods*

Bord, Janet and Colin: *The Evidence for Bigfoot*

Clark, Jerome and Coleman, Loren: *Creatures of the Outer Edge*

Crystall, Ellen: *Silent Invasion: The Shocking Discoveries of a UFO Researcher*

Fort, Charles: *The Book of the Damned*

Gethard, Chris: *Weird New York*

Holzer, Hans: *Ghosts: True Encounters with the World Beyond*

Hynek, J. Allen, Imbrogno, Philip J., Pratt, Bob: *Night Siege*

Irving, Washington: *The Sketch Book of Geoffrey Crayon, Gent.*

Pitkin, David: *New England Ghosts*

Soule, Gardner: *The Maybe Monsters*

Strieber, Whitley: *Communion*

Newspapers and Periodicals

Chatham Courier

Daily Herald (Rutland, Vermont)

Exeter (NY) *Watchtower*

Glens Falls Post-Star

Globe, The

Hudson River Chronicle

Poughkeepsie Journal

Register-Star (Hudson, NY)

Times Union (Albany, NY)

Photo Credits

Paul Bartholomew

William Brann

Susan L.

Lisa LaMonica

Margaret Mayer

Rob Morphy

Jack Bulmer

Library of Congress

Bruce G. Hallenbeck

www.ingramcontent.com/pod-product-compliance
Lightning Source LLC
Chambersburg PA
CBHW022057020426
42335CB00012B/725